Reflections on the water

The Memoirs of a North Country Fly Fisher

by

Stan Schofield

Published by Stan Schofield

First edition 2003©

ISBN 0 9545240 0 4

FOR LYNN, MY LOVING WIFE, WHO IS ALWAYS

THERE TO WELCOME ME BACK HOME.

Special thanks to Guy and Mary Britton,
for help with proof reading.

The better things of life, we know
Aren't always got for pay;
For often things worth more than gold,
Are free along the way.
The folks who fish, find happiness
In the lure of woods and streams,
While others try, but fail to find
This answer to their dreams.

(From menu at York Fly Fishers' dinner)

"No life, my honest scholar, no life so happy and so pleasant as the life of a well governed angler, for when the lawyer is swallowed up with business, the statesman in preventing or contriving plots, then we sit on cowslip banks, hear the birds sing, and possess ourselves in as much quietness as these silent silver streams, which we now see glide so quietly by us."

Izaak Walton (1593-1683) - "The Compleat Angler".

The author and three Nith Springers

CONTENTS

			Page
INTRODUCTION			2
Chapter 1	"THE BEGINNING"		3
Chapter 2	"MY FIRST JACK"		6
Chapter 3	"A GENEROUS MAN"		8
Chapter 4	"ELLIS, BRING THE NET!"		10
Chapter 5	"A WINDY DAY"		12
Chapter 6	"RACING HOME FROM SUNDAY SCHOOL" and "CHRISTMAS DAY 1934"		14
Chapter 7	"BENBECULA, MY WARTIME PARADISE"		16
Chapter 8	"MY FIRST COQUET SALMON" and "CATCH OF A LIFETIME"		19
Chapter 9	"FRIENDLY FISHING IN THE TROPICS"		22
Chapter 10	"THE LOST REEL" and "DEAD HARE"		25
Chapter 11	"WHEN ALL SEEMED LOST"		27
Chapter 12	"NITH SPRINGERS"		30
Chapter 13	"I MEET TIM"		34
Chapter 14	"THE CHALLENGE OF SUNTER'S DUB"		36
Chapter 15	"BILL STURDY, A MAN OF THE RIVERSIDE"		40
Chapter 16	"TWO TWENTY POUNDERS"		42
Chapter 17	"JOHN'S YTHAN SEAL"		44
Chapter 18	"MY IRISH GHILLIE"		46
Chapter 19	"A FIRST ON THE TYNE"		49
Chapter 20	"A DOUBLE TREBLE"		51
Chapter 21	"BASIL, A SMALL- STREAM EXPERT"		53
Chapter 22	"TWO LINCOLNSHIRE LADS"		55
Chapter 23	"A SPECIAL DAY ON FOSTON BECK"		59
Chapter 24	"AN EVENING ON THE AIRE"		62
Chapter 25	"TWO SEA TROUT UP A TREE"		64
Chapter 26	"A RED-LETTER DAY WITH MAC"		66
Chapter 27	"ONCE IN A FISHER'S LIFETIME"		70
Chapter 28	"AN INCH OR TWO MAKES ALL THE DIFFERENCE"		72
Chapter 29	"A SHOOTER'S TROUT" and "A FISHER'S DUCK"		76
Chapter 30	"THE RESTAURANT"		78
Chapter 31	"ALL WENT WELL"		80
Chapter 32	"HER LADYSHIP"		82
Chapter 33	"A MORNING TO REMEMBER"		85
Chapter 34	"THE GREAT CHANGE"		88
Chapter 35	"FOUR SPIRITS RETURN"		90
Chapter 36	"FINAL THOUGHTS"		93

INTRODUCTION

In this collection of fishing tales, I have attempted to describe a selection of the most memorable moments in almost a lifetime's passion for angling ..... my recollections of halcyon days by the water, achievements and frustrations, memorable fish and the good friends and characters I met along the way.

My abiding love for angling, kindled when I was but a child, has never left me. In my early life, wherever life's twists and turns took me, my rods usually followed, but, once war was over, I returned to my native North Yorkshire, and ever since have fished my beloved Dales rivers and, whenever the opportunity arose, journeyed northwards to pit my skill on the rivers of Northern England and Scotland.

It is my hope that my recollections of "the noble art" will not only bring pleasure to my readers, but some, I hope, will find here a sufficiency of interest, humour and stimulation to inspire them to take up the challenge and become a fisher themselves. If so, from the moment they make their first cast, they will be embarking on a journey, which could give a lifetime's pleasure.

If my tales do these two things, then I will be a contented man.

Chapter 1
"THE BEGINNING"

The ponds where it all began

Though not realizing it when very young, I was most fortunate to grow up on a farm in North Yorkshire, which enjoyed the added amenity of four old disused brick ponds, out of which clay had been dug, some one hundred and fifty years ago.

The ponds and ancient brick kiln, with walls three feet thick, were the only relics remaining to remind one of the toil and hardship of those men involved in this rustic country industry all those years ago. Well established with nature's wealth of trees, weeds and wildlife, the waters were rich with an abundance of fish: perch, pike, roach, chub and minnows and, like most inland waters, a fair share of very large eels. The ponds were a real haven for water-loving birds: mallard, coot, water hen and snipe. They appeared to live quite happily together, with the occasional quarrel only in the breeding season. There was an annual invasion of frogs, toads and newts. Insects, beetles, shrimps galore and all manner of minute life flourished.

In summer, the sky above the water was alive with dragonflies and swooping swallows. The midsummer migration of young frogs and toads in their thousands is something I shall never forget. In the adjoining meadows, skylarks, joyous in full song, reached ever upwards to the heavens.

The ponds, extending to some three acres, had a large island in the middle, with a main path leading back to the site of the old kiln. All four ponds were connected and the fish could move from one to another. Willow, alder and hawthorn were well established and so were the dense mare's-tail reeds fringing the margins of the ponds, creating a real haven for spawning fish and nesting birds. The whole scene was one of sheer beauty and rural peace, especially in the summer months.

In those now far off days, at the age of seven or eight, I looked forward to Sunday, for it was on this day that we could, in the fishing season, expect an invasion of fishers from the industrial cities of the West Riding. They came by train to the local village railway station, from Leeds, Sheffield, Bradford and other industrial towns, glad, no doubt, to leave behind the grime of the work place and to relish the peace and pure air of my countryside.

From the railway station, they would walk the good mile to the farm, carrying their large wicker baskets filled to the brim with all manner of fishing impedimenta, their long rods and nets slung over their shoulders. A noisy welcome from our two farm dogs heralded their arrival. Mother was given the princely sum of sixpence per angler for the pleasure of their day's sport. Occasionally, she would be asked to supply a pot of tea and refreshments for later in the day.

I am sure she enjoyed this change in her weekly routine and always made sure that fishers were given thick sandwiches of home-baked bread, liberally spread with homemade butter and a generous slice of home-cured ham, together with a large portion of her favourite rich sweetcake. The charge for this splendid country fare was another silver sixpence. How times have changed since those far-off days!

From a very early age, I was fascinated by the brightly coloured cork floats used by these men from the big cities. Occasionally, I would be asked to supply a few brandling worms obtained from the farm manure heap. Two pennies seemed to be an appropriate reward, with sometimes the gift of a fishing hook or float. As I got older, these gifts were much more welcome and I began to accumulate a few pieces of fishing tackle.

However, I still did not possess one of their envied greenheart or mottled-cane rods with lancewood tops. Nor did I own a polished walnut brass-backed reel and silk line. In those far-off days, such fine equipment was not available to me. Farmers and their farms were experiencing hard times and many country folk had a struggle to feed, clothe and educate their children. These were the priorities of my parents, for which I and my brothers and sisters will be forever grateful.

This lack of funds did not prevent me from fishing. A nearby wood contained several large coppices of hazelnut trees, which not only supplied us with nuts for Christmas, but for me, more importantly, the hazelnut tree grew long, slender, very straight shoots of tensile wood in lengths varying up to eight feet and more. A careful selection of the best was made and with pocket knife, a pair of pliers, some wire for rings and a reel of cotton for binding them on, the strip of hazel was fashioned into my very first fishing rod. Armed with a bobbin of Mother's best Dewhurst black cotton for a makeshift reel, a float shaped from the cork out of a medicine bottle, plus a treasured hook kindly given to me by one of our city fishermen, my first fishing outfit was nearly complete. With the final addition of a small sliver of lead cut from the farm pump spout to act as a sinker, I was all set to go. Over the years, that old pump spout got shorter and shorter, as my two younger brothers took up angling, with the subsequent demands for more lead weights to cock our home-made floats.

With my crude outfit, I would spend all my spare moments in the summers of my youth, fishing in those peaceful surroundings of my home. The fat, fighting, willing perch gave me all the joy a small boy could hope for. With a wriggling worm impaled on the hook, I would pull several loops of cotton from the bobbin in my pocket. Then, swinging my new rod, I cast the float, lead and bait into the pond. It was amazing how far I was able to cast despite the crudeness of my tackle. Even so, hooks were lost in trees, weeds and roots and often I was reduced to making my own hooks from pins Mother gave me from her needlework basket. It always amazed me how successful we boys were at landing hefty pound perch on such crude hooks. That is, until quite recently, when after some sixty years I realized that the modern barbless hook is little different from my bent pins of long ago and that worthy fish can be safely caught on a hook minus its barb. So, perhaps my very early successes were not so astonishing after all!

I was always the last to leave the water when Mother called her boys in for supper and bed. Like the perch, I was, at that young age, well and truly hooked and have been ever since.

I shall be forever grateful to those genuine, kind-hearted city anglers who tolerated my presence and who, through their generosity and patience, set me on the right road at the beginning of my fishing journey. I pray that in the tranquil surroundings of my old home and its peaceful ponds, those men, who toiled among the grimy wheels of industry in the great cities, long, long, ago, found there that little bit of Paradise they richly deserved.

Chapter 2
"MY FIRST JACK"

From the now distant memories of my youth, I can vividly recall the capture of my very first pike. I had watched other anglers catching the pike that thrived in my father's ponds, but as yet, I had not come into contact with the feared denizen of the deep.

Monday, being Market Day in nearby Thirsk, was the day Mother did her shopping for the coming week. I gave her four pence from my little tin money-box, with instructions to purchase two hooks to strong gut from Tommy Macauley's fishing tackle shop. I say "fishing tackle shop", but in fact, Tommy sold just about everything. One moment he was putting maggots into fishermen's tins and in the next minute he would be weighing out butter and slicing bacon for his lady customers. With such varied activity in his corner shop, I cannot recall Tommy ever washing his hands, but perhaps he did! He was a jovial fellow, a good fisherman and his shop never seemed short of patronage.

Racing home from the little village school, I waited expectantly for the arrival of the local market bus, bringing back all the country folk with their baskets full of the weekly provisions. Mother smiled when I eagerly asked her the question, "Did you get my hooks, Mam?" That was all I wanted to know. I could not wait to get my hands on those two little cellophane packets containing the lethal steel for my evenings' sport with the perch.

The worms had been dug up and I was away to the ponds, but not for long. Young as I was, I had to do my fair share of work on the farm. A cow had to be milked, calves fed and hay brought in from the stack outside, whilst my younger brothers attended to the feeding of pigs and collection of eggs from the old kiln ovens in which the hens did their daily good deeds. At last, I was free to hasten back to my waiting rod on the middle path between the ponds.

At the call of "Suppertime!" I baited up my hook with a large worm and cast it far into the middle of the pond. Then with a length of binder twine, I secured the rod to the "lazy-back", made from a sturdy forked branch of a willow tree. In the past, this mode of fishing had produced many a fine perch by the following morning. A lazy way to do a spot of night fishing, but, to a young boy, most effective and that was all that mattered then.

Mother's expertise with the frying pan on the open fire ensured that we boys enjoyed the culinary delights of any overnight success. On the morning in question, with the milking done, I galloped down to the ponds, eagerly scanning the surface for my bright red float. No sign was a good sign. Down the middle path I raced and saw that my rod was still tied to the "lazy-back", but not at the angle I had left it at the previous evening. The line was taut, reaching down into the deep depths of the centre of the pond, with no sign of my bright red float.

Hastily untying the twine holding my rod in the willow fork, I slowly and gently began to wind in my line, which at first came in quite easily. Then, suddenly, some fifteen yards out, the surface exploded! This was not the normal reaction of a captive perch and in that moment, I realized I had something very much larger to contend with. Surely, it must be a pike!

Trembling with excitement, I played the monster most carefully, for I was afraid that Tommy Macauley's cheap gut hook would surely be severed by the pike's razor-sharp teeth. After what seemed ages, I pulled my night's capture through the reeds and out onto dry land. Cautiously grabbing the pike and my rod, I raced home proud of my trophy.

Having made absolutely sure that the pike was dead, I proceeded to trace my precious hook, which appeared to be somewhere deep in the pike's throat, well out of sight beyond the rows of needle-sharp teeth. With my home made disgorger, eventually I was able to retrieve my hook, which appeared none the worse for its adventure.

When the pike was opened, there in its stomach was a small quarter-pound perch, but no sign of my worm! Had this unfortunate perch first taken my worm and hook, then itself been taken by the pike? It is like many happenings in fishing - a mystery I can never solve and so will never know. What I did know for certain was that I had caught my very first jack pike, weighing six pounds. Though not a monster in pike terms now, it was then, to me, at the age of nine years, a giant, if not a monster and the start of many exciting battles to come with Esox lucius, the terror of the deep.

Chapter 3
"A GENEROUS MAN"

One of the regular visitors to our ponds in the early and mid-thirties was a gentleman who, if my memory serves me correctly, came from the Middleton area of the city of Leeds. He was just an ordinary chap, who toiled in a noisy engineering works throughout the week. A quiet, softly spoken person, I am certain he found immense contentment in the peaceful surroundings of our farm and ponds. Unlike some grown-ups, he had a quality that today I admire. It was simply that he always listened to the young. With his quiet manner, he was able to converse and give confidence, which I am sure influenced me very much all those years ago.

He would always share his rod with me and he never showed annoyance at the tangles I often got in his tackle. He had no children of his own and, though I did not realize it at the time, I suppose I partly took the place of someone he longed for.

The day I wish to recall was an extremely hot midsummer day, with a cloudless blue sky and the incessant buzz of myriad insects. Swallows swooped across the heavens in their never-ending quest for food for their growing young. The blazing sun was draining the oxygen from the tranquil waters in which the shoals of roach and perch sought shade beneath the willows and alders.

Mr. Madden had demonstrated to me the art of fishing the floating chrysalis, a most effective and skilful form of fishing under the conditions of the day. His bulging keepnet was proof of his artistry and fine touch, using the most delicate gut cast obtainable. Without fail, he would release all his catch at the end of the day and any spare maggots and chrysalises were tossed into the water as a parting gift.

It was my custom to help Mr Madden undo his tackle before we parted company, he to walk the long mile back to the country railway station to catch his evening train home to Leeds. On this particular evening, he astonished me by saying, "Don't tackle down, son."

"Why not?" I enquired.

"It's all yours."

I was flabbergasted and cannot remember how I thanked him. I simply could not comprehend that all I was holding in my hands was now mine.

For several more years I always looked forward to his coming, spending many happy days together in those peaceful surroundings. Under his wing, I became a most competent and knowledgeable fisherman at a very early age.

The dark clouds of the Second World War were creeping ever nearer and, once they had broken and burst upon us, I lost for ever the friend who had given me so much that was to hold me in good stead in the years to come.

At the age of eighteen, I found myself in the Royal Air Force and for the next five years and six months, I was far away from home. Sadly, on my return home at the end of the war, my mother told me that she had not seen or heard from my old friend. I feared the worst, but still lived in hope. The years passed and, most reluctantly, I had to accept that we would never fish together again.

My memories of Mr Madden - I don't even know his Christian name - will never fade. He taught me so much, not only about fishing, but also of nature and the world outside. Most of all, I think, he showed me the inner pleasure one can get by giving generously and being patient with the young. I have, more than once in moments of reflection on all those years now gone, wondered whether or not Mr Madden had some influence on my chosen profession, that of schoolmaster.

I would, indeed, be most happy if that was so!

Chapter 4
"ELLIS, BRING THE NET!"

Looking back over the characters encountered in my early fishing days, none was more eccentric and convivial than Mr Plotkin, a most exclusive tailor with a lucrative business in Harrogate, catering for the many rich patrons in that Spa retreat.

With Ellis, his chauffeur-cum-ghillie at the wheel, they arrived with the car full to the brim with all manner of fishing rods, nets, seats and umbrellas and always, without fail, a large, green, bait can full to the brim with lively minnows. Mr Plotkin was, as ever, immaculately dressed in a tweed suit of plus-fours, highly polished tan brogue shoes, spats, a brightly-spotted bow tie and large Homburg hat.

On his previous visit to our ponds, Mr Plotkin had been twice broken by something powerful. The fish, whatever it was, had never been seen. On each occasion, his tackle had ended up somewhere deep down amongst the roots of a giant willow, with Plotkin helpless to do anything but shout, "Ellis, bring the net!" Poor Ellis had had to drop his own rod and dash round the pond, only to be greeted by a downcast red-faced Plotkin, still trembling from the excitement and exertion of the battle lost.

On this particular day, I can clearly recall helping Mr Plotkin put a new silk plaited line on his Nottingham reel. I could detect that my friend from Harrogate meant business, for the breaking strain of his new line was ten pounds and the gilt hook tied on the strongest of gut.

With a lively minnow impaled by the lip, the first cast was made. For half an hour or so, the bright red float bobbed about in the middle reaches of the deep pool. Then, just as Plotkin was about to reel in and make another cast, the float vanished out of sight. After a few seconds' pause, the spare line was slowly wound up and, when all was taut, he struck! His greenheart rod truly bent and twisted under the excessive strain and counter-strain of angler and fish. Plotkin, as was his habit, shouted, "Ellis, bring the net!" not realizing that there was I, already in the water up to my wellington tops, with his net at the ready. Out of the corner of my eye, I could see poor Ellis hurrying round from the far side of the pond. By the time he arrived at the scene of battle, Plotkin was winning the contest. With rod bent nearly double and reel creaking on the ratchet ever so slowly, the pressure was telling. At long last, the float came into view and then the cast, followed by a huge blackish, yellow, writhing mass of eel, as thick as a man's forearm. The biggest eel I had ever seen!

Thank goodness, the net was one of the good old-fashioned sort, round and large. At my fourth attempt, I had it safely in the net and on the bank. Always well prepared for such eventualities, Plotkin produced a newspaper with which Ellis, using both hands, attempted to grasp the angry, slippery eel. What a job it was, before the valiant Ellis gave it the final coup de grace.

I cannot remember the exact weight and length of this gigantic eel, but I do know that even when dead I was still a little scared of its evil-looking head and long yellow-tinged belly. I suppose that it must have weighed at least five or six pounds.

Mr Plotkin was, I think, rather overcome with all the effort and excitement, for he went to his car and produced a small silver flask which he put up to his lips several times. This seemed to calm him down and soon both he and Ellis were back fishing and at peace.

In the war years, Mr Plotkin and Ellis would use their precious petrol ration to come and fish the ponds. My mother would always give a full report on Mr Plotkin's visits, in her weekly newsletters, which she never failed to write to her sons far away on war duty.

Over the years more large eels were caught when fishing the ponds, but I am sure, never as big as the one Ellis called "The Monster".

At the end of the war, I again had the pleasure of meeting Mr Plotkin. To mark my admiration for this friendly, talented, extrovert man, I respectfully wish to record that he kindly made me my wedding suit and my new bride, a most beautiful coat. It was typical of the man that the workmanship was of the highest order. I will never forget his love and enthusiasm for his sport nor his friendship and many kindnesses to my family and I.

Chapter 5
"A WINDY DAY"

I have a feeling that for most of us the mind selects certain facts and episodes from life, which for some inexplicable reason, it never forgets. Even after the passage of many years and whether important or not, these memories do not lose their clarity, meaning or truth.

One of these early recollections that is still clear in my now ageing mind relates to the day Mr Barker, a fine arts expert and keen sportsman, paid the ponds a visit. Arrangements had been made for me to supply the worms and Mr Barker to supply the tackle to fish for the lovely perch found in my father's ponds. I can well remember running to open the farmyard gate for the gleaming, black Vauxhall saloon to pass through. All cars in those days appeared to be black. At that time, we had a small Irish terrier, Nipper. On occasion, he was prone to steal up behind any stranger and make his presence felt in no uncertain manner. I did not want this to happen to my friend. With Nipper safely tied up, the usual friendly exchanges between my parents and their guest took place.

After a short walk down the middle path of the ponds, it was clear that the gale-force wind was going to be a problem. I was, however, inwardly excited, knowing that I was to fish with a lovely split-cane rod, of far superior quality than my humble cane rod. The reel and line were also of high quality. I had seldom before had such a treat, and even then, only for a few moments, never for the whole day. I was ecstatic!

In view of the elements, Mr Barker decided to fish with the wind at his back and I, of course, followed suit. For a good half hour or so, we failed to locate one of the shoals of perch we were after. Mr Barker suggested that perhaps there was a pike in the vicinity and he may well have been correct. Even at my tender age, I was beginning to glean fishing knowledge.

After a further spell of inactivity and perhaps in desperation, my friend turned round on the narrow path dividing the ponds, faced the violent easterly wind and cast into the choppy waves. Within seconds, he would have to lift off and re-cast, as the waves were considerable and quickly took his float and tackle very near the reeds. Before he could even do this, however, his float vanished and his rod bent into the first fish of what was to become an extraordinary afternoon. The long-handled net proved a real boon, as fish after fish took avidly. His keepnet was soon full, so I brought an old tin bath down the path for the last twenty-three perch. Sport was so fast and furious that there were times when we both had a fish on at the same time.

At the end of this memorable day, Mr Barker insisted that all the fish should be safely returned to their home. He estimated they included specimens weighing well over two pounds. These were the pick of the thirty-nine fish captured in the teeth of that gale. So excited was I with my tally of fourteen fish that I had not noticed my wellingtons were full of water. With a lovely fishing rod in my hands, thanks to the kindness of my fishing friend, and the willing perch, my day had been perfect. All good things must eventually come to an end. With a last wave at the roadside gate, I ran home in squelching wellingtons, clutching tightly in my hand a bright silver shilling.

Chapter 6
"RACING HOME FROM SUNDAY SCHOOL"
and
"CHRISTMAS DAY 1934"

All those years ago, before the onset of the Second World War, I, together with my two younger brothers, Guy and Lewis, were required to attend Sunday School, like most other children of our era. Whether we liked it or not, we were obliged to don our best Sunday clothes and cycle the one and a half miles to the local village chapel. In winter, we did not mind too much, but in summer things were different, especially when Mother had promised us a picnic by the riverside. Though we had our own ponds at home in which we could fish at any time, the opportunity to fish in running water for large barbel was something very special for us. Also, the thoughts of Mother's picnic and the promise of an extra treat, a bottle each of Theakston's wonderful tasting lemonade, made the day even more significant.

On such Sundays, it was, therefore, a mad dash home from Sunday School for we three boys, followed by a quick change into our old togs and wellingtons. Then, together with Mother and her large picnic basket filled to the brim, we set off across the fields to the River Swale, some three quarters of a mile distant.

On arrival at the riverside, Mother would sit under a large pine tree, overlooking the fast flowing water. Soon we boys were tackled up and fishing hard. Mother was, I am sure, always fearful that one of us, in our excitement, would fall in and be swept away.

In that picturesque setting, we would trot our worm-baited hooks down the swift stream, expecting the home-made, red, cork floats to vanish at any moment. When they did, cries of joy indicated a barbel hooked. These rather mysterious whiskered fish put up a powerful resistance. Many of them weighed some five pounds and more. When we landed one, it was unhooked and placed in a small retaining pool, which we had created at the edge of the river.

Having laid out the food, Mother would call us up from the water to relish the prepared banquet. After the feast, it was back to fishing the river before the time arrived to return home. Removing the stones at the side of our little pool enabled the captured barbel to escape and swim away, back to their deep haunts. How good it was to see them regain their freedom at the end of such perfect days.

Finally, as the shadows of the dying sun lengthened and the evening air cooled, we gathered up our fishing tackle and with Mother, her picnic basket now considerably lighter, we wended our way homewards across the darkening meadows. Three very happy, contented, young fishers and a very loving mother!

My love of fishing had grown apace. For some time, I had yearned to possess a fly rod and try my hand at fishing with an artificial fly. I nagged my parents, but my pleas fell on deaf ears, for times were hard. As Christmas approached, I renewed my appeals .....

..... I will never forget that historic moment in my life, Christmas Day, 1934. Through the good offices of Santa Claus, I became the fortunate owner of a brand-new Allcock split-cane rod, reel and silk line to match, with two gut casts and four gleaming trout flies. The brightest of those treasured flies was a Butcher. This had the honour of being tied to the point of my cast, which I had soaked in my breakfast cup of tea. I had done this, having read in an old fishing book that tea not only softened the gut, but also made it invisible to the fish.

On that Christmas morning, I raced down to the ponds, only to find that the whole water surface was under a sheet of thin ice. With no trout in the ponds, my aim had been to try out my new outfit on the large chub and perch. In my immature mind, I envisaged them, even in midwinter, just waiting for my fly. However, not to be denied, I stood on the reed-frosted edge and, still full of excitement, I made my very first cast with a fly upon the gleaming ice. For half an hour, I was in my own little world, before the frost got the better of me.

Since those far-off days, many hundreds of trout have been drawn across my outstretched net, yet never has a season commenced without my mind reflecting on that first cast I made over the ice. This moment saw the birth of my life-long love of the art of fly fishing.

Footnote:

Little did we know at that time in our young lives that within a matter of five years, we would be at war with Germany. Three of Mother's sons would find themselves far away from home. The land between our small farm and the river, which we had come to know so well, suddenly changed its appearance. Hedges and woodland disappeared to be replaced with concrete runways from which giant Halifax bombers and their largely Canadian aircrews flew on their dangerous nightly missions over Europe. The tranquility of our youthful scene sadly became a thing of the past, but even with the passage of time, my memories of glorious carefree days by my father's ponds and the River Swale remain undiminished.

Chapter 7
"BENBECULA, MY WARTIME PARADISE"

Looking back over fifty or more years of my life, I can recall with clarity and pleasure so many angling experiences which have remained fresh in my memory long after other, perhaps more important events, have been forgotten. Some such memories come from a time during the war when I was working in radar, stationed at Borve Castle on the small, windswept, yet beautiful island of Benbecula in the remote Outer Hebrides.

My first impression on landing was one of complete bleakness. Not a tree in sight! Only a single row of stubby telegraph poles, following the line of the narrow winding road, broke the flatness of the landscape. The ever-constant wind and rain, which swept in from the Atlantic Ocean in that first January, did not help. I well remember writing my first letter home to my mother, who must have gained the impression that her son was well and truly in a foreign land and not in part of the British Isles.

With the eventual arrival of more spring-like weather, my thoughts turned to fishing and I ventured forth to survey the many lochs to be found throughout the island. I was pleased with what I discovered. By this time, I had made the acquaintance of a local crofter, Roderick Macauley, his brother Donald and his elderly mother. Roderick worked the farm with only his horse to assist him on this thinly soiled land. Donald, on the other hand, was much more refined, with a degree in agriculture from Leeds University. His work, as an agricultural adviser working for the government, took him away from home to the mainland and the other Hebridean islands.

I was extremely interested in their way of life, so different from my own. At first, I was treated with caution, but eventually the ice was broken and we became firm friends. The bond of friendship was sealed after I offered to milk Roderick's two cows for him when he was laid low with a severe bout of influenza. With no light in the cow byre, I had to do the milking in darkness.

To my eager enquiries concerning the trout fishing, I got the answer, "Och, plenty good trout!" This was all I wanted to know, and I wrote home immediately, requesting that my fishing gear be sent on to me. Roderick, a burly fellow who loved his food, was also keen for me to have a go for the wild duck, geese and rabbits, which lived on the island. At his suggestion and prompting, I purchased a 12 bore shot gun from one of his crofter friends. Roderick agreed to look after the gun for me, as I was not allowed to keep it in my service quarters.

In due course, a long, mysterious-looking box arrived labelled "Glass. With Care". Harry Richmond, the local joiner back home in Yorkshire, had made it especially for me. No nails were used, only brass screws. Harry had made a very sturdy job of the container and the rod, folding net and tackle were in perfect condition, despite their long journey.

At once, I prepared for my first day's fishing. As the island was pitted with lochs, I did not have to travel too far to make my very first cast. When the day dawned for my first venture, the weather was not conducive to fly fishing. The chilly wind, with the possibility of rain did not, however, prevent me from striding out across the peaty coarse terrain to the loch, which Roderick had suggested I try first. He was not too impressed with my light, split-cane rod and tiny trout flies and suggested that I fished the worm.

I was determined to fish the fly and so I made my very first cast into the sheltered bay of a loch. Covering the water for an hour without success, I was beginning to think he might be right. This first little loch had failed to produce a rise for me, so, following a sheep track across the peat bog, I arrived at a long narrow stretch of water. At my fourth or fifth cast, there was a swirl on the surface and my first Hebridean fish was hooked. I was thrilled! The trout, safely in my net, would, I thought, weigh just under a pound. It had taken the top dropper, a Greenwell's Glory. With a Mallard and Claret on the middle dropper and a Silver Butcher on the point, I was now confident that more sport was in the offing. Stimulated by this success, I went on to take another three trout of similar size, before increasing heavy rain forced me to retrace my steps to Roderick's croft. I think I surprised him when I emptied my two brace of Benbecula trout onto a large dinner plate. That evening his respect for my "bit of stick" was somewhat enhanced when he tucked into fried trout and boiled potatoes, with home-baked bread and butter.

Whenever possible during the next few months, I was out with the rod and gun and, though not being able to appreciate my sport fully because of the war, I did have a wonderful time catching many fine loch trout, the largest weighing just over two pounds. Rabbits were plentiful and the crofters, who allowed me to shoot their land, were always pleased with the contents of my game bag.

 I think it was sometime in mid-July when I had the joy of catching my first ever sea trout from a tidal loch. Fishing tackle was extremely difficult to obtain and my first few sea-trout flies were most valuable to me. Despite my care, losses were inevitable with large swathes of seaweed growing in profusion in many parts of these sea lochs. In addition, some of my gut casts were showing signs of wear and tear. I can well recall sending a £1 postal order to Allan's of Edinburgh, requesting sea-trout flies and, if possible, a gut cast or two. By return post, I received a small package containing three sea-trout flies and a letter apologizing for the severe rationing of their dwindling stock. This excellent firm politely pointed out that I was in credit to the value of fifteen shillings. I never did make use of that credit!

On my off-duty days, I would often have lunch at the Creagory Inn, the only hostelry on the island. Here for half a crown I partook of simple but nourishing food and drink. In addition, I was given much information on the fishing, where to go and the best lochs to fish. Several crofters suggested the worm, but I steadfastly stuck to the fly.

That summer was one of the most enjoyable of my whole life. Many sea trout were caught. I even managed to send three fish home to Yorkshire. Wrapped in damp reeds inside a wooden box obtained from the cookhouse on the camp, these fish arrived in Yorkshire within two days, via Scottish Airways to Glasgow and then on by train. My mother and father had never tasted sea trout until this surprise package arrived at their door.

Those lovely sea trout, newly up from the sea and wonderfully pink fleshed, were accepted most gratefully by the crofters, who had made it possible for me to enjoy the thrills and riches of their remote island home. With the fishing season over at the end of September, Roderick made the necessary arrangements for me to shoot over his neighbours' land. Rabbits were plentiful and, with mallard and the occasional greylag, I was always made welcome, especially by the wives of these hardy crofters.

In those dark days of war, at times I almost forgot why I was in uniform. I had come to love this rugged island and its people. No man could have enjoyed more his stay in their midst. It was the saddest of days when I had to say "Goodbye", for I had found great happiness and peace amongst those friendly crofters and their wonderful island of Benbecula.

Chapter 8
"MY FIRST COQUET SALMON"
and
"CATCH OF A LIFETIME"

In the dark days of the Second World War, after my duties on the Isle of Benbecula in the Outer Hebrides, I was posted to a radar station in Northumberland. On my arrival, I had to explain to the officer in charge of the Guard Room that the long wooden box marked "Glass. With Care" contained nothing more sinister than my personal fishing tackle. After the obligatory inspection, I was allowed to keep my precious gear in my room. I am sure the vivid description of my fishing exploits on the wild and windy Hebridean island swayed the officer's decision in my favour.

It did not take me very long to find out that the River Coquet, a salmon river, was but some five miles distant. On my first free day, I borrowed a bicycle and cycled as fast as I could to the pretty town of Warkworth, with its splendid castle towering above the river. For the last half-mile or so the road ran alongside the river. My first impression of the river and the quaint little port of Amble at its mouth, made me eager to see more of the Coquet.

Leaving my cycle in a clump of nettles by the castle ramparts, I walked down the path leading to the river, which almost encircled the town. A short distance upstream, on a bend in the river, I chanced upon a lone angler. By the length of his fly rod, he was obviously a salmon fisher. Much later, I found he was fishing a favourite salmon lie called Swan Neck Pool.

I had never had the opportunity to fish for salmon, nor the chance to talk with anyone who had. I introduced myself politely and soon found myself conversing with a fine middle-aged gentleman, a Mr Walker, who told me he had a small fishing tackle business in Alnwick. He was a most charming fellow, who, recognizing my eagerness and enthusiasm for fishing, invited me to accompany him on the following Thursday, providing I was able to arrange my Service duties. He came down from Alnwick most weeks of the season and always kept two fly rods ready tackled up in a riverside cottage, inhabited by an old lady, who guarded his rods. These were hung on nails in the wall leading up the staircase of that humble dwelling.

I shook hands with my newly found friend and hastened back to camp. That evening I wrote a letter home requesting my mother to post up to me the alloy fly box in my bedside cabinet. This box, containing some forty or so salmon flies, I had purchased from Macpherson's of Inverness. I had no idea as to their worth or usefulness as far as the Coquet was concerned, but

I felt I ought to have them for my first experience of salmon fishing. On the following Tuesday the package arrived and that evening I inspected each and every fly in detail. To my dismay, I found that more than half the flies, though beautifully tied, had gut eyes, which on closer inspection were perished and useless. However, the remainder had metal eyes and were usable. On the arranged day, I was away on my borrowed bicycle to meet Mr Walker at the old lady's cottage. If I remember correctly, Mr Walker, a dapper little man, had a gleaming black Rover car, immaculately polished.

It was only a matter of taking the rods down and carefully negotiating them through the cottage doorway and then off we went upstream towards the pool where we had met the previous week. At this point the river appeared fairly sluggish, at least so I thought, having been used to the faster running rivers of the Yorkshire Dales. What I did not realize was that the river here was affected by the tides. At high tide the fresh water was held back and the pool was consequently much deeper. As the tide receded, so the river's natural flow was increased with the downward pull.

I had never had a fourteen-foot rod in my hands before. I watched Mr Walker for a short while. Then, taking up that lovely split-cane fly rod in my two hands, I made my first ever cast upon a salmon river. Though I was a most proficient caster of a trout rod, this technique was rather different. In due course, my confidence increased and so did the quality of my casting. The country was at war, yet here I was, completely at peace, engrossed in my efforts to catch the "King of Fishes". I was stimulated to greater effort by the sight of a fish leaping, some hundred yards downstream. The day passed without a take, but we did witness a more fortunate angler, who hooked and grassed a gleaming twelve pounder.

Late in the afternoon, we returned to the cottage and put the rods up the stairway. I thanked my host most cordially. What a grand person he was, for he gave me carte blanche to come down whenever I wished, provided I always left him the other rod should he also come to fish. And so, for several weeks, whenever the calls of Service life would allow, I spent many happy hours fishing the Warkworth beat of the Coquet. My one and only success came as I fished just below the old road bridge, which spans the river to the north side of the town. I am sure I did everything wrong. The fish led me a merry dance, on two occasions threatening to go through the arches of the bridge, where it would most certainly have broken me. Thank goodness the synthetic gut cast was equal to the tensions that fish and my inexperience put it to. I do not know how long I fought the salmon but, at last, I was able to draw it between two seaweed-covered boulders, get my hand in its gills and finally heave it onto dry land. I had caught my first salmon! Alone, I gazed at its gleaming blue-silver flanks and powerful tail for several minutes, my heart pounding and my mouth dry. With shaking hands, I unhooked and weighed it. It registered ten and a half pounds on my spring balance. This freshly run fish will remain forever in my memory.

At the end of the day, I took the fish and offered it free to the manageress of the exclusive Sun Hotel in Warkworth. She accepted this gift most warmly and invited me to dine when my fish was on the menu three days later. It proved to be an excellent meal in the austere times of war.

This was to be my first and last Coquet salmon. Though I paid several more visits to the river, I was not fortunate enough to experience again the thrill of a screaming reel and leaping Coquet salmon.

Soon after this milestone in my fishing career, I had cause, I know not why, to visit the local dance hall in the mining village of Red Row. Though I did not know it at the time, I was about to make the catch of my lifetime. A most beautiful girl in Royal Air Force uniform caught my eye. At the end of the dance, we walked back to camp. It was the starting point of a life-long friendship together. Despite my posting abroad to India, Burma and Malaya, we never lost touch. At the end of the war, some three years later, we fell in love and duly married. We are still happily together some fifty years later. Surely this must be the finest catch ever of this fisher's life!

When we first met

Chapter 9
"FRIENDLY FISHING IN THE TROPICS"

In the dark days of the war, the forced move from the wild rugged island of Benbecula to Northumberland, with its beautiful River Coquet, had turned out to be a fortunate transfer. Despite the vagaries of Service life, my fishing on this fine river had been most enjoyable. From the fishing point of view, I therefore felt disappointed when the day came that I was told my services were required overseas. Where to? I was soon to find out, but not before rumours had placed my destiny in Iceland, Canada, Australia, the Azores and Africa. All proved false.

My eventual arrival into Bombay harbour, with its new scenes, strange noises and intense heat, could not have been more removed from the comparative quiet of my two previous postings. I was a member of a mobile radar station. At the time of landing, the Japanese still occupied the whole of Burma and there were fears that they would invade India by travelling up the coast to the Bay of Bengal. We had to cross the sub-continent to play our part in combating this threat. A long, tedious train journey right across the heart of India brought me to the great Brahmaputra River. This runs from its source on the far side of Tibet, beyond Mount Everest, through the mighty Himalayas and finally ends its long journey in the Bay of Bengal. A gigantic river when in spate ...... and gigantic when not!

For the first time throughout the long journey, thoughts of fishing came back to me, especially at the sight of a group of young, partially naked Indian boys, half swimming, half wading, fishing in the dirty brown water, using a primitive net made from what looked like strips of bamboo. The minute shrimps and small sardine-sized fish they caught were, I suppose, their staple diet. These little urchins, surrounded by poverty, were obviously happy in their work. I particularly envied them their extreme agility in the water. In this, and their never-ending search for food, they reminded me of little brook trout, darting hither and thither.

A brief stay in Chittagong gave me the opportunity of playing some inter-service football. Three trophies on my sideboard are an ever-constant reminder of those happy far-off days.

Down the Arakan and Burmese coasts, I found much to interest the angler. The art with which the hardy fishers threw out their circular nets and the intense delight expressed on their sun-tanned faces at a good or unusual catch, made me realize that anglers over the world have much in common. Black, yellow or white, are we so very different? Certainly, I felt no different and, whenever possible, would try my own hand with their crude, yet effective, nets and traps. The language barrier could be a problem, but the odd few words and signs were enough for our mutual friendship.

After some months, the success of Allied troops in Burma meant that the threat of invasion had receded. My long return journey took me down the Brahmaputra, across the Ganges to Calcutta and back to Bombay, then down to Poona, Bangalore and finally Madras. This gave me a real insight, not only into the geography and vastness of India, but also an understanding of the millions who struggle to survive in this often harsh, arid and sterile land.

From Madras, I sailed across the Indian Ocean to Singapore, arriving a few days after the Japanese surrender. Our mobile radar station was attached to Changi airport, at the rear of the infamous Changi Jail. Despite the horrors of the Japanese occupation, now it was over, I was able to see and appreciate a different side of this land. I had the opportunity to spend many hours among the native anglers. Fish, so vital to both the Malay and Chinese people, were found in abundance in the warm, shallow, coastal waters. I was fascinated, like a child, with the brilliant colours of the tropical fish.

One old Malayan, with whom I fished, insisted I called him "Joe Louis". Why? I never could find out, for he was a small skinny fellow, weighing no more than seven stone! My permit to fish with him in his sampan was the giving of a few cigarettes. I thought this well worthwhile, considering that boat, boatman, tackle and bait were included in the bargain.

In Joe's flimsy sampan, exposed to the Equatorial sun, I became expert at catching fish the native way. Our tackle consisted of some four or five yards of strong cotton thread with a hook attached, which we baited with shrimp. This was thrown overboard and allowed to sink. The line end was tied for anchorage round our big toes. Both left and right feet were used. Thus, we became our own living fishing rod.

Yet another experience was night fishing for giant crabs. Perhaps "fishing" is not the correct term to use, for my tackle consisted of a straight bamboo shaft, on the end of which I attached an old meat fork. This implement was used to spear the crabs. Our fishing was done in the dark with the aid of torchlight. Whilst I held the speared crab down, my young native companion, Che-king, a tough, wiry, Malayan boy, put his foot on the crab and I would then release the spear and carry on with the hunt. Che-king completed the capture by reaching down and grabbing the crab trapped under his foot. He then popped the crab into a wicker basket slung over his shoulder. Perhaps it was just as well I did not understand too much of his native tongue, for I always knew when the crab had come off best. His toes were certainly tougher than mine!

When the time came for me to leave, those simple, contented folk were sorry to see me depart and the feeling was reciprocated. I am sure I had become a better person for knowing them. Through the medium of angling, we had become friends. Consequently, though happy at the thought of coming home, I was more than a little sad when I shook hands with my tropical fishing friends, knowing that I would never see their smiling faces again.

Che King – My Malayan fishing friend

Chapter 10
"THE LOST REEL" and "DEAD HARE"

Though rather sad to leave my fishing friends in Singapore, I was eager to return home to England and especially my native North Yorkshire. At last, the great day arrived and I boarded the "Arundel Castle" bound for England. Eventually, we docked in Liverpool on a bitterly cold day in November 1946, but so glad to be home.

In the intervening years since my departure, the land between our family farm and the River Swale had been transformed into an aerodrome, from which giant Halifax bombers had taken off and flown many missions into Europe. Gone were the fields, hedgerows and woodland I once knew so well. They had been replaced by a vast open space of flat grassland, dissected by broad straight runways, now silent. No longer, the roar of mighty bombers filled the air at dusk each evening. No longer had they to set out on hazardous missions over Europe, some never to return.

As I looked over the open expanse, I thought back to my last days before I was called up to the war in July 1941. I remembered bidding farewell to my school pals, some of whom I would never see again, for soon they would pay the supreme sacrifice. I remembered the few weeks of grace before my turn came to don uniform and leave my home, my parents, my dogs and the freedom of the countryside. In those last days I fished the peaceful glides and streams of the River Swale whenever possible, staying by the waterside until dusk. Many times this lone figure galloped all the way home in darkness. I knew every field, tree, fence and gate along the way.

On my very last trip to the river before my departure into His Majesty's Forces, I can recall hastening back home too late to help my father and younger brothers with the milking and foddering of the livestock. Inspecting the contents of my fishing bag later that evening, to my great dismay, I discovered my reel, a birthday present from my parents, was missing. The following day, in broad daylight, I retraced my steps of the previous evening, but nowhere along the route was there a sign of my missing reel. I feared it was lost forever, for on the morrow I was to leave home.

The next five years found me, like millions more, engaged in the war and the lost reel was the last thing on my mind. Now, as I looked over the deserted airfield, I noticed that wild life was slowly returning to the countryside and nature was beginning to shape the landscape once again.

The country pursuit of hare hunting on the disused aerodrome became a feature of my rehabilitation in this immediate post-war period. On this particular day, my brother Guy and I were out with our two dogs, Prince and Duke, in the heart of the aerodrome. Suddenly a hare sprang up and dashed across the grassland. We slipped the leads off the dogs' collars and the hunt was on. Twisting and turning, the hare gave the two dogs a gallant chase, but the odds proved simply too much and Prince, the fastest sporting dog I have ever known, made the kill.

Within moments, I was on the spot to ensure a clean and speedy death for the hare. Amazingly, near the hare's hind legs, my eyes caught sight of a dull metal cross in the long tufty grass. I bent down and, to my utter astonishment, I picked up my long-lost fishing reel! I recognized it immediately for it was in remarkably good condition, considering it had lain there for seven years on this grassland between the runways, unfound, and exposed to all the elements. The bone handles, walnut drum and brass work seemed little the worse for wear after such a long time. More surprisingly, the drum would still turn. The machine oil, with which I had treated the reel all those years ago, had been a lifesaver, but credit must also go to Allcock's of Redditch, the makers of such a fine reel. The silk line on the spool was completely rotten, crumbling in my fingers.

Some years later, I gave the reel to a young angler who certainly used it during his initiation into the wonderful world of angling. I would not be at all surprised if this most durable survivor, purchased in 1937, was still in working harness, now over sixty-five years old!

What odds, I wonder, would anyone give on such a coincidence? Strange certainly and certainly true!

Prince – Monarch of all he surveys

Chapter 11
"WHEN ALL SEEMED LOST"

In the immediate post-war years, my life was full with new responsibilities. Lynn and I married. I went to college and qualified as a teacher. I was fortunate to obtain a post teaching boys sport and physical education at a local secondary school. Despite rationing, life was returning to something like normality.

Though extremely busy, I longed once again to take up my fly rod. Whenever time allowed, I would dash off to local rivers. If I could afford them, I added to my meagre collection of trout flies. A visit to the local fishing tackle shop was something to look forward to and eventually my fly box became reasonably full of all the local Yorkshire patterns of the day, enough to keep me happy for the immediate future. I fished my local rivers, the Swale and Ure, joining two fishing clubs. Later, I became their secretary and remained so for the next forty years of my life.

Soon, I was also fishing further afield and I took up salmon fishing, never having forgotten the thrill of my first salmon on the Coquet when I was stationed in Northumberland. I looked forward with gusto to my annual three days at Easter on the River Nith in Dumfriesshire. Like most Scottish rivers at that time, this river enjoyed a fine run of spring salmon. Unlike conditions today, I seldom returned home without at least one pristine Springer in the car boot. One early trip in the mid 50s was only for two days, but what success I had: eleven salmon, five fresh fish, the best eighteen pounds, and six kelts, including three very large grey-backs, late runners, which were safely returned, after giving me great sport.

In the August of this same year, something quite drastic happened to me when fishing the River Swale below Catterick. I had had an early tea and planned to fish for grayling, which the river held in goodly number. It had been a warm humid day with the threat of thunderstorms. This evening the runs and glides of this most pleasant stretch of water were dimpled with the soft rises of countless fish. After half an hour of frustration, with fish after fish ignoring the several patterns I presented to them, I at last had a positive take and the tiny dark Needle fly began to work in my favour.

Rumbles of thunder higher up Swaledale brought premature darkness to the evening. Quite suddenly and ever so silently, the air in the river valley turned quite chilly and the river lost its vibrant life. The rise had gone and, with two brace of fine grayling in the bag, I left the river in the approaching gloom and, crossing the meadow to the car in the nearby lane, I untackled my gear and headed for home.

No sooner had I put the car in the garage, than the heavens opened and the thunderstorm broke and raged. Sheets of lightning and rumbles of thunder echoed far up in the Pennines to the west. Emptying my fishing jacket pockets, I suddenly realized that my one and only fly box, full of all the flies I possessed, was missing. Twice I searched the inside of my fishing bag, the seats, floor and boot of the car. Even the pockets of my trousers were turned inside out, but all to no avail.

I sat down and went through in my mind all my movements during the evening's sport. I mentally fished the water again step by step. Then it suddenly came to me. I remembered placing my fly box, still open, on a flat stone at the side of the river, fully expecting, in my haste and frustration, to have to change my fly yet again. I knew the exact spot and so decided to get up early the next morning and return, hopefully to retrieve my precious box. It would be a round trip of sixteen miles.

As dawn was breaking, I drove on wet roads void of other traffic. Crossing the dew sodden meadow, I hastened down to the pool where I hoped to find the box of flies. Alas! The overnight storms in the upper dales had brought the river into spate and the flat stone was now a good foot under water. There was no sign of my fly box and flies. They were gone, now no doubt, well on their way to the sea. To this young schoolmaster, this loss was a calamity.

However, at this time in my life, I had been enjoying reading several angling books loaned from the local county library. In one of the books, I remembered reading of a similar incident befalling a fellow angler, who then resorted to tying his own flies, as he could not afford to buy them.

The name "Veniard" had stuck in my mind and I soon found out that this very reliable firm, catering for the fly tyer, still existed in Thornton Heath, Surrey. It did not take me long to obtain their catalogue and helpful leaflet on the simple basics of fly tying. It was the start of a whole new world for me and I have now been tying trout and salmon flies for over fifty years. Thank you Veniard's for your wonderful service over all these years. I have derived immense pleasure in mastering the art and being able to create beautiful and effective flies from feather, silk and fur. I have made countless friends happy by starting them on the way to becoming competent fly tyers themselves. On the riverside, how enjoyable it is to offer a fellow angler one of your own creations, knowing that it will give that person pleasure in testing it out and finding that occasionally it works.

With all the changes since those early days, the modern fly tyer has a wonderful array of materials at his disposal and I am sure that he, with a little imagination, will enrich his days, when his own creation is cast upon the water and the reel sings a merry tune.

I must admit that at the time, I did miss my small box of flies, but the resultant mastery of the fly-tyer's art has been a huge bonus and has given me immense satisfaction ever since that fateful moment on the banks of the River Swale when all seemed lost. There is nothing that matches the sense of achievement I feel when I catch a trout, grayling or salmon on a fly I have tied myself.

Chapter 12
"NITH SPRINGERS"

Easter was always a time of keen anticipation for this particular schoolmaster, who for several years in the fifties and early sixties, looked forward to a few days' fishing on the River Nith in Dumfriesshire, Scotland. In these post-war years, the Nith enjoyed a fine run of early spring salmon, which gave some wonderful sport.

The journey from Yorkshire, via the A66 trans-Pennine route, was often at this time of year an eventful one, with a real mixture of snow, fog, rain and low cloud, especially in the region of the wild bleak summit of the upper-Pennines at Stainmoor Pass, where winter lingers and is loathe to give way to spring. On these annual visits, I was often accompanied by a fellow fisher, usually my good friend, Ian Hutchinson. In those days, our route from Scotch Corner took us through Bowes, Brough, Appleby, Penrith and Carlisle, crossing the border into Scotland south of Gretna Green. We glanced at each river we crossed, Eden, Border Esk and then the Annan, eager to see the state of the water. Finally, we reached Dumfries with its fine, predominantly red stone buildings. Running through its very centre was the River Nith. At this point, the giant cauld, a local name for the weir, with its leaping salmon was a sight for any fisherman's eyes.

After a brief stay at this thunderous cauldron, we continued up the valley of the Nith to the small town of Thornhill. Here, at Mr Coulthart's shoe shop, we would pay our dues for the privilege of fishing the Mid-Nithsdale waters, extending for three miles downstream of Penpont Bridge. To reach our final destination, we crossed the bridge and entered the peaceful village of Penpont, notable for its lovely church and fine steeple.

At the Albury Guest House we were always made most welcome by Dick Robinson and his good wife, who was responsible for satisfying the inner-man, with her superb cooking and for her attention to our homely comforts. Welcoming fires in the lounge and dining room made us feel completely at home. Albury was in those far off days a real haven for we salmon fishers.

Dick, himself a first class salmon fisher, especially with the fly, would, after a hearty meal, bring us up to date with all the recent happenings on the river. He would describe the state of the water and, with his expert knowledge, outline our own prospects for the next few days. He told many tales of local characters, men like "The Cobbler", who perhaps caught more salmon than anyone else, using his own special techniques! Talk would invariably include tales of battles with the Nith's autumn running grey-backs for which the river was renowned. Dick, an exile from Yorkshire, would describe them thus: "As long as railway sleepers, with tails as big as a shovel." Having myself experienced several encounters with these back-end giants, I feel that I cannot better his description of these magnificent fish.

Sadly, our trips to the Nith came to an abrupt halt with the onset of the salmon disease, Ulcerative Dermal Necrosis, usually abbreviated to U.D.N. In a very short time, it nearly wiped out the whole stock of fish, with the River Nith one of the most seriously affected rivers in the British Isles. Happily, Nith has now regained some of its former glory, but I feel, despite this progress, I will never see again the wonderful runs of spring fish leaping the cauld in the heart of beautiful Dumfries. I can, however, still hope!

Whenever in the company of old fishing friends, it is inevitable that memories of halcyon days from the past come flooding back. I can still recall most vividly my first encounter with these early Springers over fifty years ago. Having travelled up to Albury the previous evening, with my good fishing companion, Ian, we set forth to fish Porter's Pool, from which Dick Robinson had caught a lovely nine pounder the previous day. With late winter's snow still clinging to the tops of the Keir and Lowther hills, we arrived at the riverside to find the water in excellent ply, with some ten inches of extra water on the stone marker on the opposite bank. It looked an ideal spinning water. Dick had suggested that we give the Devon minnow first trial. The sun was up and already the early morning frost was disappearing from the grassy bankside.

At this time of year, salmon are often slow to react after a frosty night and consequent lowering of water temperature. Having fished the lovely pool down twice with no response, we rested awhile in the fishing hut. I changed my blue and silver minnow to a golden Devon. After a welcome coffee, we were back at the head of Porter's. Eleven o'clock it was when, a third of the way down, I was into my first Nith fish. Even at this time of year, it was not unusual to hook the kelts, making their way down river to the Solway. As the fish bored deep for some considerable time, I wondered if it could be a kelt.

However, it was not long before I had my first sight of the fish, some fifteen yards downstream. "It's a Springer!" Ian yelled. After several more minutes of defiance, the battle was won and I was able to bring the fish into quieter water, where Ian was ready with the net. A pristine spring fish weighing eleven pounds, straight up from the sea, was my first of many fine fish caught over the years on this wonderful river.

Hastening back to the head of the pool, Ian took the lead down, with me following some forty yards behind. Halfway down, where a small stream entered the main river on the opposite bank, my luck was again in. The line tightened and, with a firm strike, I was into my second salmon of the day. In the powerful stream, this fish bored deeply with a constant shaking of its head, the possible sign of a big fish. After a prolonged battle of gaining a few yards, then loosing a few yards, I was able to bring the fish to my side of the main stream. Despite feeling that I was gaining ground, neither Ian nor I had had a good view of the fish. Suddenly Ian shouted, "It's a big one!" My heart raced even faster at this and I became increasingly worried, as the salmon had been on for some twenty minutes and was now ever so slowly dropping back towards the powerful draw of Caulback Pool below. Should it slip back much further, I feared I would lose it, but I could do little to stop its downward course.

At this dangerous moment in the proceedings, a local farmer suddenly came upon the scene and immediately brought his knowledge of the pool to my aid.

"Walk back into the field!" he instructed. "Keep going!" he shouted. The rod was bent double and the line humming with tension. I was sure that the hook would tear out. "Keep walking," he again urged and, without any hesitation, he strode into the water, which at this point was waist deep. "Hold it there!" he yelled. Suddenly the line went slack, my rod straightened and for a split second, I feared the worst. The sight of Ian reaching down to the farmer to take the net, with a silver bar of salmon safely in its mesh, eased the pressure on my pounding heart. When my saviour was safely back on land, we weighed the fish - eighteen pounds eight ounces!

Introducing himself, Mr Stitt, wet through to the skin, was as delighted as I was at the capture of such a fine salmon. For his valiant effort on my behalf, I pressed a note into his hand and offered to drive him home, but, "No," he replied, "I have the sheep to attend to", and off he disappeared over the embankment.

"Now that is a good shepherd," I thought. From that day on, we were the best of fishing companions whenever we met on the banks of the lovely Porter's Pool. Mr Stitt himself was a good fly fisher and over many seasons, I enjoyed his company and friendship.

The following day I had the good fortune to capture another eleven pounder to crown my first visit to this fine salmon river. Three never to be forgotten perfect Nith Springers!

Poor Ian, he hooked a beautiful fresh fish, which I estimated to be at least twenty pounds, only to lose it after six or seven minutes' battle, when his brown and gold Devon minnow was torn from the fish's mouth, as it suddenly leapt clear of the water. In that split second, it was all over. How I felt for him in that agonizing moment of truth and disappointment. Another day that could well be my misfortune, for over the years, since that first foray, I too have experienced all too often the feeling that Lady Luck has deserted me.

That, we have to accept, is salmon fishing!

Chapter 13
"I MEET TIM"

Though my occasional salmon fishing trips North of the Border were the highlights of my fishing year, most of my free time was spent eagerly fishing for trout and grayling in our own Yorkshire rivers. I spent many hours on the Swale and Ure and ventured further up the Dales, especially into Wensleydale where the Ure is known by its old Danish name of Yore.

One evening, whilst casually reading a copy of a Yorkshire monthly magazine, I came across a fishing article written by someone with the nom-de-plume of "Broughton Point". He struck me as a man who not only knew a great deal about fishing, but also came over as a man who loved nature. For some compelling reason his article made me want to meet him.

It did not take me long to find out who "Broughton Point" really was. I wrote to him, enclosing a small sample of my own flies for him to try out on his native River Aire. In addition, I invited him to come for a day's grayling fishing on my favourite stretch of the River Ure. The invitation was immediately accepted and, on the following Friday evening, I was at the railway station, waiting for the Leeds Express to arrive.

There was no mistaking Tim Wilson as he came squeezing through the barrier, with two rods, landing net, fishing creel and case and with a pair of green thigh-waders slung round his neck. That first evening there was much talk and laughter, as I tied for Tim a few of his favourite flies and gave him a picture of the water we were to fish the following day.

I always think that October is the best month for fishing the fly for grayling, providing the weather is fair with some autumn sunshine. After a hearty breakfast, we were off. The sun was already shining as we headed westward, with the car boot crammed full of fishing tackle, waders and lunch basket. The day could not be more perfect for the joys ahead. The grayling and trout were already rising by the time we had arrived, walked down to the river and tackled up on the bank of a delightful glide, fringed on the opposite side with willow and alder. The deep run, two thirds of the way across, was an ideal haunt for the grayling. It was not long before we were all set. A slight breeze ruffled the water very lightly. "Perfect conditions," I thought.

Tim commenced fishing with a Rolt's Witch and I put on one of my favourite Yorkshire flies, a Treacle Parkin. Within minutes of starting, Tim's rod was bent into his first grayling of the day. I followed him down the pool and in no time at all we were in action. The odd trout was hooked and carefully returned to the water. So too were the grayling, all in prime condition. I think Tim alone accounted for well over a dozen by lunchtime and I was not far behind with a tally of nine grayling and two trout. Tied on size sixteen hooks, our two flies proved most attractive to the fish that morning and neither of us had cause to change our fly, until we couldn't put it off any longer, as they were beginning to look very bedraggled.

After a quick lunch, we were back fishing the lower pool of deeper and slightly slower water. Tim changed his fly for a tiny Green Insect, with a sparse honey dun hackle. I changed to a Sturdy's Fancy, a capital fly for both trout and grayling and a favourite Ure pattern.

On that afternoon, the grayling were even more obliging and we lost count of the number of grand fish that provided us with superb sport. We decide to keep a brace each, returning all the rest to live and fight another day. "Her Ladyship" had done us proud and we both agreed that this had been a perfect day, cementing a friendship that was to last for many years to come. Tim was not only a true master of his craft but also a perfect gentleman and a friend I will never forget.

Tying flies with Tim

Chapter 14
"THE CHALLENGE OF SUNTER'S DUB"

In my early years of teaching boys the many arts of sport and sportsmanship, I would, as a treat for a chosen few, forego one week of my own summer holidays to take a dozen or so keen and eager young anglers up into the heart of Wensleydale. To reach our destination, a pleasant campsite well secluded above the pretty village of Bainbridge, we had to take the Dales train from Northallerton. Sadly, this line is no longer in regular use for the public. With cycles safely in the guard's van, bulging rucksacks and fishing gear stored on the spacious racks, we left behind on the station platform, a small group of waving parents. We were on our way!

Through the ever-changing countryside, the little train chugged along its single track, stopping at all the country stations on its ever-westward journey up the dale and valley of the River Ure. Beyond Leyburn, the green hedgerows of the lower dale gave way to sturdy dry-stone walls, stretching up into the fells on either side of the valley floor. From here, upstream to its headwaters, the Ure, named originally by the Romans as the Urus, is known by its old Norse name, the Yore, a name I love.

On reaching Askrigg station, we left the train, and, with all our impedimenta, cycled the short distance to Bainbridge, first crossing the River Yore that we were to fish in the days ahead. At the village shop, whilst I ordered the necessary provisions for our stay, the boys took the opportunity to stock up with their favourite sweets.

We cycled over the stone bridge spanning the gurgling River Bain, a tributary of the Yore, flowing from Lake Semer Water. We then pushed our cycles up the extremely steep hillsides and at last were there. The campsite was in a quiet meadow and had the luxury of a small cookhouse with a Calor gas stove, a long table, benches and a cupboard to keep our stores, cutlery and pots and pans.

On that first evening, we returned to the village, where I was able to purchase the necessary permits, enabling us to fish for the rest of the week. We walked back along part of the river before heading up to the campsite and our tents. Soon we were settled down for the night. Up early next morning, and after a hearty breakfast, the boys were keen to start out for the river. Our holiday had really begun.

Within ten minutes, we were on the riverside and happy. That evening, after a long day by the river, we sat round the cookhouse table and under the flickering light of two stable lamps, the day's catch of trout and grayling was cooked. With some very crude chips and bread and butter, followed by tinned pears and peaches, our ravenous appetites were satisfied and we slept well.

The week would pass all too quickly, but like all good things, it had to end. The boys returned home to regale their parents with stories of fish caught and lost and their adventures. I would like to think that those few days spent together in that peaceful setting made us all the more understanding, tolerant, responsible and willing to help each other. The boys became better sportsmen and their skills with rod and line were enhanced. Their obvious enjoyment, smiling, sun-brown faces and the impressions they left on all those they had contact with during their week on the banks of the Yore, made me a happy man.

Sunter's Dub, a large, deep, fast-flowing pool, situated a short distance below the confluence of the Bain and Yore held a fine head of both trout and large grayling. It was quite natural for this stretch of the river to attract the attentions of many more anglers than other parts of the river. Here both the resident trout and grayling were very well educated and difficult to catch, especially in the low, clear waters of high summer. Even the local experts found them difficult to catch. No matter what fly was used, very few fish could be deceived and lured into taking one's offering, no matter how delicately it was presented. Late evening was perhaps the only time the big fellows could be enticed to take, for they were, even at this time, extremely wary.

Meeting Dick Chapman, an old friend and local expert, we discussed the fish of Sunter's Dub. Dick, a retired schoolmaster from Bradford, who had come back to the dale on retirement, had spent much of his leisure time on the riverside and was an expert fly fisherman. What a grand fellow he was, witty and lively in conversation and vastly knowledgeable on the wiles and ways of Yore trout and grayling. With all his local expertise, even he had concluded that tempting big fellows in Sunter's Dub was virtually impossible in the low clear waters of summer. Only in a flood and coloured water did the local lads, with their worming gear, catch the old stagers ...... and only then if they were lucky.

Through careful observation over several seasons, I had noticed that the fish in Sunter's Dub did rise, but that the fly they sipped was so tiny that it would be impossible to get a hook sufficiently small to copy the caenis, yet effective in hooking and holding in the mouth of a sizeable fish. After much discussion with Dick about the problem, it was agreed that I bring my fly-tying equipment down to the Rose and Crown Inn the following lunch time and there we created half a dozen fancies with which I could challenge the residents of Sunter's Dub that very same evening.

And, so it was with careful planning that we met on that sultry summer's evening to do battle. I could not have had a finer outfit for the task ahead: my favourite Charles Ritz Fario Club rod, matching reel and floating line. The latter was mounted with a nine foot tapered cast with an extremely fine point, upon which I carefully tied one of my specials, a small light-green body and one turn only of a small honey dun hackle.

All was set, with a gallery of youthful eyes, under the control of Dick on the opposite bank, observing every movement I made. The sun, though low and hidden beyond the western hills, still gave the scene a sharp brightness. I dare not wade into the water, for the disturbance would be an irredeemable mistake, nor dare I stand up in case of skylining.

A nice rise in the central stream was my first target. At my second cast, the fish rose and was hooked. On the opposite bank, Dick had great difficulty in keeping the excited boys quiet. Within seconds, I recognized the telltale twisting movements so characteristic of the grayling. Just as I was about to unclip my landing net, the grayling dashed down into the fast rocky water at the tail of the dub and, alas, my fly came catapulting back!

However, despite the loss of the first fish, I was reasonably happy in the knowledge that part of my challenge had been successful...... the fish had been induced to take my creation. Drying the fly, I cautiously moved up the bankside a few yards, for I had noticed a steady riser close to the bank and under the branches of a large sycamore tree. This looked much more like a trout. I waited for the fish to show again, for I realized that I would have only one chance in such a confined and difficult lie. My fly would have to fall within inches of the lowest branch and no more than a foot from the steep bank side. A few false casts and out it went. "Too near the bank," I thought, but no, for, before I realized it, the reel was singing and out in the centre of the dub a fine trout leapt clear of the water. Before I could take any further part in the proceedings, this fish too had torn away from the flimsy hold. This is what Dick and I had feared.

Nevertheless, I was now more determined than ever to prove to Dick and my young observers that the hook hold could be mastered. It was, I thought, an excellent opportunity for me to show my young angling students how to tackle and overcome a difficult challenge. These lads had great respect for me and I felt that I must not let them down.

By now the light was beginning to loose its power and I felt it was safe to stand up, as I had a darkening background behind me. It required a long cast to cover the next fish, rising consistently a yard out and in the shadow of an overhanging bough. Once again, the Fario Club did its stuff and my cast point straightened out some two feet above the last rise. A silent swirl and I was into my third fish of the evening.

This time I would be as delicate as possible and, with both encouragement and much advice from the gallery, I played the fish with the utmost care. Eventually I slid the net under a grand three-quarter pound trout.

Success at last! From the reactions of my companions, I could see that they too enjoyed the conquest. With daylight fading, I felt I could use a slightly larger fly, so on went a Treacle Parkin, one of my favourites. Carefully skirting the large tree, I crept down again to the water's edge and waited. There, not ten yards upstream, was the slightest of dimples. Again this fish was hugging the near bank and, as I could not make a normal back cast due to the over-hanging sycamore, I made a roll cast. At my third attempt, a sliver of silver on the water's surface. A take! I tightened on a much larger fish, which shot past me and towards the roots of the big tree. With gentle persuasion, I eased it out and into the main stream of the pool, where it bored deep before dashing up upstream. Gradually the fish tired and its runs shortened. Unclipping my net, I drew this gallant trout towards me, and victory was mine. The trout, a deep bronze, weighed just over a pound.

My brace of trout that evening weighed well above the average for that part of the Yore. They were fine examples of native fish, which I am sure to this very day, bring out the best in those that dare challenge them in their safe haven beneath the old sycamore tree of Sunter's Dub.

Chapter 15
"BILL STURDY, A MAN OF THE RIVERSIDE"

I cannot really remember when first I met William Sturdy of Masham in North Yorkshire, as I seem to have known him for the major part of my adult life. What I do know is that Bill, as he is affectionately known by his many friends, is one of the nicest chaps that I have met in all my sporting life. He is a real countryman. Now retired, for the major part of his working life, he was the respected custodian of several beautiful miles of fishing in the middle reaches of the River Ure.

Following in the footsteps of his uncle and cousin before him, Bill cared for, developed and extended a trout hatchery to cater

Bill and Mick on river patrol

for the growing demands from the increasing numbers of fly fishers in the post-war period. He was a true and loyal servant, who, year in, year out, faithfully produced high quality trout to stock this delightful stretch of the Ure.

Bill loved his work and could always be relied upon to be on the riverside to assist all who fished the water, especially the elderly and the young tyro. He readily shared his knowledge and expertise with these lucky anglers. Many of them have him to thank for putting them on the right road to becoming masters of the fly-fisher's art.

He is not only a fine fisher of the fly, but is also extremely proficient at all other forms of angling. He loved a day's pike fishing and forays on the banks of a salmon river. His fly-tying skills were renowned, especially for his North Country spider patterns: Snipe and Purple, Waterhen Bloa, Orange Partridge, March Brown, Greenwell's Glory, Olive Dun and Pheasant Tail. Sturdy's Fancy, a fly well known to anglers in the North Country, designed by Bill's grandfather, has stood the test of time. Originally created as a grayling fly, it has, for nearly a century, proved itself to be also an excellent taker of trout.

In the Centenary Year of the club he has served so well, I was asked to design a special fly to be given to members and their guests attending the Centenary dinner, where the fly was named Sturdy's Centurion, as a fitting tribute to Bill.

Bill has many stories of his beloved riverside, but one I rather like has nothing to do with fishing ..... but shooting. He was on Dallowgill grouse moor on an extremely hot August day, loading for no less a celebrity than Mr Bing Crosby. During a lull in the shooting, Bing left the butt to walk to a nearby stream to quench his thirst. On his return, he remarked how deliciously cool and refreshing the water was in the tiny stream. Bill decided to do likewise on this sweltering day and, walking a little higher up the stream, was about to kneel down to slake his thirst, when he saw the rotting carcass of a dead sheep in the water. On his way back to the shooting butt, Bill pondered awhile. Should he tell Bing or should he keep his grim discovery to himself? Not wishing to spoil Bing's obvious enjoyment of the day, he remained silent and Bing remained a happy man!

The River Ure, a fine trout river, is also a haven for grayling, producing wonderful sport in the extended fishing season. In the mellow sun-flecked waters of autumn, Thymallus is in the prime of condition. I have spent many days with Bill fishing the Hackfall streams for the resident grayling. Tiny Red Tags, Treacle Parkins and Sturdy's Fancies proved irresistible to them. We were following in the footsteps of the great Thomas E. Pritt, author of the classic "The Book of the Grayling". Over one hundred years ago, he caught his finest brace of grayling in Sandybed Stream, where Bill and I have had so much joy with a fish rightly called "The Lady of the Stream".

Sadly, in the 1960's, the few salmon returning to the River Ure brought with them the dreaded U.D.N. disease. Though not infecting the trout population, the grayling, a member of the salmon family, was severely affected, with the result that the stocks of this wonderful sporting fish were decimated. At the height of the infection, for days upon end, Bill would scoop hundreds of dead grayling out of his beloved river. Thankfully the river is now slowly recovering, but it will be many more years before the glory days of Bill Sturdy's tenure return to the clean, vibrant, dancing waters he jealously guarded, nurtured and loved. He was, and always will be, a true fisher's friend and respected man of the riverside.

Chapter 16
"TWO TWENTY POUNDERS"

It has always amazed me how that pirate of fresh water, the pike, can live for many years undetected, even in a well-controlled trout fishery. With such a rich food supply, this predator can grow to a huge size. There is no doubt that he, or more likely she, will be well trained in the art of camouflage deception and will have become wily over the years. Tales of big pike fascinate, as they usually involve the violent and sudden death of their prey, and their very existence is the stuff of legend and mystery.

Nevertheless, it came as a real surprise to this ardent trout angler when he discovered that Esox lucius was residing in the middle of his club's trout preserve. If the trout were to survive and reach maturity, such a veritable monster had to be removed without delay. As I was the secretary of the fly-fishing club in question, I felt responsible and at once set in motion plans for the removal of this uninvited guest from our water. Capture was all the more urgent, as the annual restocking with some one thousand twelve inch trout was imminent.

Basil Gilbank, a good friend and expert pike fisher, was called on to assist. He promised to go the following evening, assuming he could obtain a few herrings from the local fishmonger. A pike will invariably remain in the same location, provided his larder is well stocked. Knowing the exact swim, Basil prepared his tackle with care. Two treble hooks on a wire trace were attached to his twelve-pound nylon line. He selected his herring bait and all was ready.

The monster had been residing in a small back-wash, within some five or six yards of quiet water, away from the main stream, shielded by the battered remnants of an old, storm-ravaged willow tree. With an accumulation of flotsam at its base, this was a typical pike lair. With the evening sun at his back, Basil took care that his shadow did not fall across the small area of water into which he wished to cast the herring bait. With a plop, in it went. Giving the herring a few feet of slack line, allowing it to sink, the trap was set. Now, all Basil had to do was to keep out of sight, watch and wait, with eyes on the limp nylon line at the point where it entered the water, waiting for any telltale signs of movement. Five minutes went by, then ten. The tendency at such times is to get impatient, retrieve the bait and make another cast. Experienced in pike behaviour, Basil waited, knowing that a large pike is a cautious and wise scoundrel. Unlike the brash and impetuous younger jack pike, the leviathan tempers a voracious appetite with wary vigilance and discretion.

Suddenly, the line was twitching, a sure sign that the dead herring was being mouthed. No need to hurry. Basil waited until the line began to straighten out, then struck. The battle was on! No doubt about it, this was a big one. A strong dash out into mid-stream, gave Basil time to move downstream and apply pressure to keep the pike away from its willowy den. Despite some violent head shaking and frantic efforts to throw the hooks, Basil's tackle held firm and the fish began to flag under the constant pressure of his powerful fibreglass rod. The steely point of the gaff marked the end of the pike's gallant battle for freedom. No longer will those vicious teeth put fear into the hearts of lesser creatures that dared to enter Esox's watery domain. We felt that at last peace would return to that stretch of water. At least, that is what we thought!

The following week, I spun a large pike spoon through that very same spot, past the willow tree and on to the end of the pool. Here, on the very lip of the run off into the next stretch of water, I was taken with a resounding thump. My eight-pound line of several years' vintage was stretched to the utmost in preventing the pike from going into the next reach of the river, where more willow trees would prevent me from following. I would certainly have lost the battle had this occurred. Slowly, I coaxed the fish upstream and, as I drew it towards me, it opened its gills like two barn doors, a fearsome sight. Eventually, I beached it on a gravel spit and the priest did its work.

Yes, it was another monster pike. I wondered, was this fellow just arriving to take over the residence of the recently departed, or had they been joint owners of what must have been a very lucrative property? We shall never know. Sufficient it is to record that my pike weighed twenty-one pounds five ounces and Basil's tipped the scales at twenty-two pounds ten ounces.

This delightful stretch of trout water still has this little quiet corner. The old willow tree remains, fully adorned with its collection of debris brought down by the floods. Basil has, however, ensured that no new, would-be owners of this quiet backwater have remained tenants for long.

Even so, with our combined experiences of the elusive Esox lucius, neither Basil nor I would be too surprised if, at some future date, another giant emerges from this quiet little corner!

Chapter 17
"JOHN'S YTHAN SEAL"

After fishing for over seventy years, I have come to realize that the only certain thing in my sport is the uncertainty. It is always dangerous to be too dogmatic, as the unusual and unexpected are part and parcel of the fisherman's day. There is an explanation for most of these incidents, but not always. Sometimes something happens that defies logic, as the following story illustrates.

Some years ago, my good friends, John Kellett and George Fawcett, were fishing the Udny Arm's waters of the River Ythan, north of Aberdeen. Their annual pilgrimage was to the small town of Newburgh to fish the estuary waters of the River Ythan for the exciting sea trout that abound in this unusual tidal fishery.

On this particular day, John was fishing the Mussel Beds, a favourite pool for sea trout, when suddenly, fifty yards upstream, there was a huge commotion in the water. A seal had chased and caught a salmon in the shallows. Seeing the angler so short a distance away, the seal let go its hold on the fish and vanished out of sight. The tidal current brought the dying fish down to John, who quickly scooped it up in his landing net. It was a beautiful fresh fish, with only a deep gash in the shoulder. His friend, George, fishing close by, witnessed the whole incident and he remarked what a lucky so and so J.K. was, thanks to a friendly seal.

In time, the incident was forgotten, until the following year, when the same two anglers were speeding northwards and again looking forward to their week's sea-trout fishing on the Ythan. Jokingly, John remarked, "I wonder if my friend, the seal, has another salmon lined up for me."

"Not b..... likely," George quickly retorted, "he has one for me this year!"

The following morning, refreshed by a good night's sleep and fortified with an excellent full breakfast, the two anglers set forth to fish their favourite Mussel Bed pool. As those who fish this estuary know, the rising tide is viewed with great expectancy, with the possibilities of a fresh batch of fish entering the river from the sea, a quarter mile distant. Already, fish were being caught by fellow anglers lined up at intervals along the sandy banks of the estuary.

High tide came and went. The tide began to recede. As it did so, the outward current in the main bed of the river increased its velocity. Sport had been good, for both angling friends had fish on the bank. In mid-afternoon, the water above Mussel Beds suddenly erupted and a seal rolled. To their astonishment a repeat order of the previous year's salmon was slowly unfolding before their eyes. There was no further sign of the seal, but a salmon slowly floated downstream ..... towards John! He quickly scooped up his second seal salmon, a smaller fish than last year's, but, nevertheless, a lovely eight pounder with sea-lice. In all probability, this fish had come in on that morning's tide.

Poor George could not believe what he was seeing. He could only mutter, "You lucky devil!"

Forever afterwards, whenever the conversation focused on salmon and sea trout, John's story would be told and retold. The odds of this most unusual happening must be immense. George was convinced that J.K. had some form of hold on the Ythan seals.

I wonder ...... could he be right?

Chapter 18
"MY IRISH GHILLIE"

In the war, when I was stationed in the Outer Hebrides, I had to fly down to an airfield in the south of England. This gave me my very first bird's eye view of Ireland. It was a lovely clear summer's day. Looking down, I was enthralled by what I saw below me: the vivid greens of the land, wild rugged hills, shimmering loughs and the winding silver threads of many rivers. They left a lasting impression on my mind. There and then, I vowed that, God willing, I would return to explore at closer hand at least a small part of the Emerald Isle.

Some twenty years later, there I was, with my wife, Lynn, driving off the Irish Sea ferry at Dun Laoghaire. We were on our way to the beautiful valley of the River Blackwater in the counties of Cork and Wexford. We were on holiday and free to do as we pleased. I had planned a few days' fishing for salmon on the Blackwater. Lynn, a very keen artist, was eager to get out her brushes and canvas. In between, we hoped to visit Killarney, the city of Cork and the attractive little seaport of Cobh, the birthplace of Lynn's father. Here she hoped to research her family tree.

On the drive down to the Blackwater, we were pleasantly surprised by the light volume of traffic on Irish roads, a real treat after the congestion on the roads from Yorkshire to Holyhead. In Ireland, donkey carts and pony and traps were often more numerous than cars. During our brief stops along the way, we were impressed with the warmth of welcome and the hospitality we received.

Our hotel could not be bettered and we quickly settled in. I fished the Blackwater for the next three days with no success. I still had not caught my first Irish salmon. The river was at summer level, but I was pleased to hear that rain was forecast and I kept my fingers crossed. Lynn, happy at her easel, was spoilt for subject matter to sketch and paint. We visited Cork and then Cobh, where we had some success, in the limited time at our disposal, in tracing Lynn's Donovan family line. My wife was delighted. Another day we visited Killarney and Lismore Castle.

On the penultimate day of our holiday, I was offered the chance to fish an exclusive and private stretch of estate water, with the added service of a ghillie. After weighing up our dwindling finances, I agreed the extra cost and so, leaving my wife to paint near our hotel, I was away to meet my guide, some ten miles distant up the river. Twice I had to ask for directions, but, without too much worry, I was on time to meet Patrick, my ghillie. We met at his cottage gate and introduced ourselves.

We were soon on our way to the water, a short distance away. Parking the car behind a stone wall in the corner of a small field, I unloaded my gear and put on my thigh-waders. To my great surprise, my ghillie insisted that he carry all my tackle, rods, net, fishing bag and lunch basket down to the river, which was a short walk away through a pine wood. I was allowed to use my wading staff down the steep track.

The river looked in splendid ply, with a few inches of extra water, tinged the colour of whiskey. In no time at all, Patrick had both my fly rod and spinning rod tackled up. I showed him my fly box and asked him to select the fly we should use. On the spinning rod, I attached a two inch golden Devon minnow.

My local expert suggested I initially try the spinner. Picking my way carefully to the head of the pool, I made my first cast. As I slowly worked my way downstream, Patrick pointed out all the likely taking places, where such and such a person had had success earlier in the season and even years ago. Arriving at the tail end of the run with no sign of a fish, we walked back to the top of the pool and I changed to a fly rod.

It was a beautiful stretch of water to fish the fly, with plenty of blue aerial space to put out a long line. The size eight, orange, shrimp fly looked most attractive in the slightly peaty water. I was in my element!

Half way down the glide, I was taken by a fish that shot powerfully downstream, making my reel chatter. I stumbled out of the water and hurried to follow along the bank, to try to stop the salmon's bolt back towards the sea. Patrick was by my side, net in hand, all the while giving me excited instructions as to what I should do and where the hidden dangers were in this deep rocky pool.

After the first frantic surge, things settled down and I was gradually able to coax the fish away from the lip of the pool below. Eventually, we had our first glimpse of the salmon. It looked like a fresh run fish and so it proved to be, when, with a dip and a lift, my ghillie had it safely in the net. I had caught my first Irish salmon! I was delighted and so was my friendly aide, who applied the coup de grace. On my little spring balance, my catch weighed eleven and a half pounds. Now was surely the time for a celebratory drink! Patrick then hung the salmon in a tree, well off the ground. He assured me it would be safe.

After a hasty lunch, I was eager to restart fishing. We walked upstream to the upper beat, another delightful stretch of water. I fished with the spinner for some time, but to no avail. Changing again to the fly rod, I slipped in at the head of the pool. Here the water was both fast and deep. Wading carefully downstream, with the water dangerously near the top of my thigh-waders, I was glad to have the help of my trusty wading stick. Nevertheless, I was able to cover all the water. Working up a casting rhythm, I felt happy and at one with my surroundings.

A third of the way down the run, the line straightened, the rod bent and I was into my second fish of the day. My elation was, however, a little premature, for within no more than a few seconds, the line went slack. Reeling in, my fly was still there, but alas, not the salmon.

The time simply flew by and my day ended with no more success. I was not too downcast, for I had enjoyed every minute on this memorable stretch of water. When the time came to leave, we cut the salmon down from the tree. Patrick again insisted on carrying my tackle, together with the salmon, back to the car. During my time on the water, we had worked in perfect harmony. We had found time to talk and he had told me a little of his life, its joys and moments of sorrow. A family man, he was worried about his fifteen-year-old twin girls, who had just left school. They had no prospect of work out there in the country. They were to leave home to find work in the big city of Cork, thirty miles away. Like all good parents, Patrick and his wife, were concerned for them.

Returning to his cottage, we were greeted by his wife and five children, including the twins. The salmon was removed from the car boot and Patrick handed it to the twins. They took it to a nearby pump and washed it spotlessly clean, before laying it carefully back on the hessian sack in the boot of my car. It was a perfect fish.

I shook hands with my ghillie and pressed his just reward into his rough palm. He had made my day memorable in so many ways and the gleaming salmon was but an added bonus.

I drove back to my hotel a contented man.

Chapter 19
"A FIRST ON THE TYNE"

Over the years, I have built up an extensive fishing library. Some books, written over one hundred and fifty years ago, give glowing, graphic accounts of wonderful runs of salmon up the River Tyne. It was rightly considered to be the premier salmon river of all England. Sadly, with the coming of the Industrial Revolution and growth of Newcastle upon Tyne, the river became a cesspool for domestic and industrial waste. The throat of this fine salmon water was choked by the thoughtless outpouring of vile effluent. The river died and the salmon was virtually wiped out.

However, in more recent years, there has been a serious effort to rectify matters and, despite the loss of some spawning grounds at the head of the North Tyne, with the building of the Kielder Reservoir, the river is slowly returning to life. With a gigantic clean up of the river mouth and vastly improved sanitation systems, salmon now have a much better chance of reaching the sea as young smolts and returning two or more years later to their place of birth as mature salmon.

A modern fish hatchery at Kielder is capable of producing thousands of young salmon parr, which are introduced into the headwaters and eventually go to the sea as smolts. It is hoped that these fish, together with the natural river-bred stock, will bring the Tyne back to its former glory. Today, the signs are most promising and the future looks bright.

Not too long ago, I received an invitation to fish the South Tyne a few miles above Hexham. With an early departure, Basil Gilbank, my fishing companion for the day, and I were on the river by ten o'clock. With salmon not the earliest of risers, this was a good time to start.

As we tackled up, we were delighted to see two salmon, showing in the pool we were to fish. The water was running some six inches above normal, so we decided to first try the spinner. Basil mounted a Mepp, while I put on an Abu Salar spoon. We walked upstream to the head of the run, where the water raced down a deep rocky cut.

 Following Basil down the pool, I felt a keen sense of anticipation as I cast and worked my spoon across the current. Within minutes, a fish took my Salar spoon in a most savage manner. Seconds after my strike, a massive salmon leapt into the air, giving Basil, some few yards away, a perfect sight of its enormous size. "A forty pounder!" he shouted. A moment later, the line went slack. Dejected and still trembling, I reeled in, but to my surprise, the spoon was still attached to my trace. On inspection of the treble hook, I found that one barb had been snapped off. The biggest salmon I had ever had on my rod and line was gone!

Since then, Basil and I have often talked about this fish. Both of us still have a vision of this monster, leaping out in a huge spray of white water. Both of us still agree it could have been a forty pounder!

Though somewhat dismayed at loosing such a large fish so early in the day, I still was optimistic. Replacing my damaged spoon, I tied on an identical lure and we continued to fish down to the railway bridge that crossed the river some three hundred yards downstream. With no further offers, we decided to rest the pool for a while and proceeded to fish below the bridge. Here the river was much wider. Though not so attractive, later we learnt that it was a favourite holding pool. However, after an hour's hard fishing we had nothing to show for our efforts. We decided to return to the car for refreshment and a pipe of tobacco.

Rejuvenated, we returned to the scene of our morning's excitement and dismay. Again Basil took first cast. Whilst he was coming to the most likely stretch of the stream, I began to fish the smooth run in the tail of the upper pool. This had not been fished in the morning. To my astonishment, I was solidly taken by a fish right on the lip of the run off, a most unlikely spot for a salmon. But there was no mistaking it was a salmon, for in no time it raced about fifty yards upstream into the deep quiet water of this very wide pool. The reel chattered as the fish rushed relentlessly on, getting nearer and nearer to a massive clump of debris held fast in the water by the roots of a willow tree. As yet, the fish had not surfaced and, for a moment or two, I wondered if by some unusual coincidence, I had hooked the giant I had lost in the morning.

Applying all the pressure I dare, we at last got a glimpse of the fish as it swirled far out in mid-stream. With its head down, it bored deeply for some minutes, but gradually I was ever so slowly recovering line. Walking backwards out of the water, I at last brought the fish into the shallows, where Basil was waiting with the net. Within seconds, the fish was netted and brought to dry land. The gleaming fresh run fish tipped the scales at fourteen pounds. I had caught my first ever Tyne salmon. This was a very special moment for me, particularly when I recalled the books I had read as a youth, which told me that the Tyne was dead.

The "King of Fishes" has returned at last to the Tyne valley and the waters of this lovely river can sing again. Since my very first encounter with the Tyne salmon, I am delighted to know that the salmon and sea trout have continued to flourish, returning this once dead river to vibrant life, making it once again the premier game fishing water in England. Long may it be so.

Chapter 20
"A DOUBLE TREBLE"

The afternoon was bright, much too bright for good fishing, I thought, as I dashed home from school. I checked that rods, fishing bag, net and waders were in the boot of the car. A quick change into more suitable clothes was followed by a hastily devoured tea of cheese sandwiches, garnished liberally with sliced onion and all washed down with a glass of cool milk. Nothing better to start an evening's fling at the trout and grayling with my good friend, Henry Thompson, who I knew would be waiting impatiently by his front door. I was running late, but I had not bargained on an unexpected injury to one of my pupils, whose eyebrow had come into contact with a cricket ball. His injury required the insertion of four stitches at our local hospital, followed by a two-mile journey to the boy's home, with all the involved explanations to a worried mother.

Henry loved his fly fishing and I enjoyed his cheerful company. Having collected him, we were soon on our way to fish the Swale at Ellerton. The river was low and clear with its bones showing more than usual. Tackling up, we decided to walk to the lower reaches of the beat and then fish back upstream.

Dry fly was the order of the evening and Henry started with his favourite winged Greenwell's Glory. I had my own preference, a small Treacle Parkin. This would be my choice if ever I had to select one dry fly only to fish the rivers of Yorkshire. I always fish it dry, but I do know of anglers who catch their fair quota with a sunken version.

Grayling were steadily rising on the smooth glides and for the next two hours, we were at peace with the world around us. Both trout and grayling were in responsive mood. As dusk approached, it was our custom to change to a wet cast of three lightly hackled spider patterns, which would be fished down the rough stickles and fast runs of the upper water.

With darkness quickly creeping upon us, sense of sight gave way to that of feel and touch. I well remember the exact spot, which, on many occasions, had given us excellent sport. The long, narrow, but deep run was fringed with willows on the far bank. At the tail of this pool, the river flattened out and it was here that fish congregated at dusk. Having fished down the willows and caught only a couple of under-sized grayling, which were returned, we arrived at the hot spot.

As darkness deepened, it was time for our final fling on this balmy night. On my very first cast, I had an immediate telltale pluck. I tightened and found myself with a jerking taut line ..... a good fish by the feel of it.

However, something was not quite right, for there were two swirls on the surface of the smooth glide. I realized at once that I had not one, but two fish on my cast. Henry decided to net the far fish and I would net the one nearer me. In the semi-darkness, this we managed to do, only to find out very quickly that the point fly was attached to a third fish!

Here we were with a fish in each of our nets and a lively trout splashing madly on the surface. By its actions, it was the largest of the three. There was nothing we could do, but gently wade backwards in the hope that we could beach this third fish. This manouvre was successful and a pound trout was carried quickly up the bank. We unhooked the two fish caught on the droppers, a half-pound trout and a grayling of similar weight. These were returned without delay, to live and fight another day. The larger trout was duly dispatched and it joined one of a similar size in my bag to make a nice brace to take home.

Now it was Henry's turn to have a final fling, for I had had all the sport I could wish for. He went back a few yards upstream. The fish were still dimpling the glassy pool. He cast his team of Orange Partridge, Waterhen Bloa and Purple Snipe. I remained well back on the bankside, but the singing of his reel prompted me to unclip my net and hasten forward. "I think there are two!" Henry shouted excitedly.

"Take it easy," I said. "Beach them if you can."

Henry carefully walked back away from the water and, nearer and nearer, the fish were brought towards the bank, splashing vigorously in the shallows. At last, the first fish was on dry land, followed by another. Then, to our utter astonishment, a third fish was beached!

"Well, I'll be damned," spluttered Henry, dropping his pipe in the excitement of the moment. A large chub, a two pounder, and a smaller one were unhooked and returned to the water. However, the third fish was a good trout, the biggest of the evening. This was soon safe in Henry's bag.

In all the excitement, we had not realized that a blanket of silver-grey mist had descended upon the water and all was now quiet. We untackled our rods by the light of the car headlights and compared our catches. Closing the car boot, we took one last glance back towards the Swale, but all was shrouded in darkness and mist.

Oddly enough, it was not until the following morning that I realized how remarkable the previous evening's events had been. Probably never again in my lifetime would I witness the catching of six fish in two consecutive casts, by two different anglers, in the same pool, and on the same night. This most unusual experience convinces me that there are times when truth is stranger than fiction.

Chapter 21
"BASIL, A SMALL-STREAM EXPERT"

Some fifty years ago, Major William Parrington of Kirby Sigston Manor invited me to fish his lengthy stretch of water on the little River Codbeck, which draws its waters from the Hambleton Hills above the moorside village of Osmotherley. Over some twenty miles, the river wends its ever-changing course down to join the River Swale, a few miles below Thirsk. I had already fished the lower stretches at the kind invitation of Dr Donald Sinclair, the Thirsk veterinary surgeon, who was a member of the Codbeck Fly Fishers' Club and, who was later to be known world-wide as "Siegfried", the senior partner to James Wight, alias "James Herriot".

Major Parrington's invitation was brought to me by his aide, Basil Gilbank. Basil knew that I tied my own flies and he kindly gave me two patterns, which he told me were the only two flies I needed outside the Mayfly season. The first and most important was the Kill Devil Spider, a Derbyshire favourite and the second was a dry Iron Blue Dun. Basil gave me a detailed account of the water and his own method of fishing the Kill Devil Spider, which was nearly always upstream. On this initial meeting, it became clear that Basil's knowledge of the water and successful tactics were unsurpassed.

Since this first meeting, Basil and I have been the best of friends. We have fished together in many parts of the British Isles and now, even in our old age, enjoy a day together with the fly rods.

When my day arrived, Basil and I walked across the meadow to the little road bridge over the Codbeck. Looking upstream, we saw the gentle dimples of feeding trout. I requested that Basil have first cast. Standing well back, I soon realized that Basil was in his element and that I was privileged to be seeing a master at work. Watching any expert at work, commands respect and Basil was no exception.

Treading ever so gently up river, he cast with a shortish line. In no time at all he had hooked and landed a lively half pounder. Short, delicate casting was vital for success, as many fish were only three or four yards away. Being able to cast with either hand gave Basil a real advantage on such an ever-meandering watercourse, with sharp over-hung corners and bends. Many a good fish had made its home beneath the deep under-cut banks.

To hurry on such a challenging stream means failure. Watching Basil, an angler of consummate skill on such waters, I was determined also to master the art of small-stream fishing. Often Basil would bring his Kill Devil Spider, which he fished just below the surface, back downstream fractionally

A tricky cast

faster than the current. This ploy would often result in a lusty fish dashing out from the over-hanging bank and aggressively taking the Kill Devil. Since that day, I too have experienced success using the same tactic.

With alder and willow lining much of the bankside, care had to be constantly taken with the back cast. A rod of eight or nine feet in length is adequate, but even this is too long to cast into several of the overgrown tunnels. A short leader of four to five feet with a four pound point is ideal for the confined spaces found on this stream.

Now I began to fish. Already a very competent caster of a fly, I quickly adapted to the new challenges of this water. It was not long before I was netting my own fish. And so began my love affair with small stream fishing.

Over the following years, I have enjoyed many a glorious day's fishing with Basil. I still admire his expertise on the challenging confined spaces of the Codbeck with its ever-game trout.

The adage "Practice makes Perfect" is certainly true for the angler who wishes to glean the utmost pleasure from fishing the fly for the residents of a small stream. But perseverance will bring great reward, for this is fishing at its very best.

Chapter 22
"TWO LINCOLNSHIRE LADS"

Fishing the River Avon, pronounced "Arn", the main tributary of the mighty River Spey, I met two grand chaps from Lincolnshire, Jim Barton and Jack Sharpe, who over the following years became good friends. Sporting rivers and fishing hotels are the ideal combination for the blending and cementing of lasting friendships amongst we fishers and so it proved on this occasion in the Delnashaugh Hotel at Ballindalloch. Our first get together in the hotel lounge over after-dinner drinks was the start of a long friendship.

Coming from the flat lands of Lincolnshire, where trout streams are rare and salmon rivers non-existent, these two fine fellows made up for this deficiency at home by enjoying fishing forays to distant parts. Throughout that first week of our meeting, they were the heart and soul of the hotel's party. Their jovial banter, humour and enthusiasm never dimmed, even at the end of a scorching-hot fishless day.

Prior to our parting at the end of the week, we exchanged addresses and telephone numbers, promising to meet once again at the Delnashaugh Hotel a year's hence. With our final handshake, I asked Jim and Jack if they would like, in the coming spring, to visit Yorkshire for a weekend, fishing on my favourite River Ure. They both readily accepted and we parted happily to make our separate ways home.

And so it was, on the Friday evening of the second week in May, Lynn, my dear wife, had the table all set for the arrival of my two angling friends from Lincolnshire. From our correspondence during the long winter months, I knew they were looking forward eagerly to fishing the fast-flowing, well-stocked stretches of the Ure. Through the good offices of friendly landowners, all arrangements had been made to try and ensure my guests would have some exciting sport. The weather forecast was for a fair weekend with warm sunshine and so all was ready.

Over pre-dinner drinks, talk inevitably turned to fishing and I was able to brief them on what to expect over the next few days. Later in the evening, the conversation turned to salmon. We had already booked our joint week's fishing on the River Avon at Ballindalloch for mid-August, so anecdotes of past experiences were aired and prospects for the coming visit discussed.

The next morning the sun was shining as we set forth on the fifteen-mile journey to the River Ure. Parking the car beneath the shady boughs of a large tree, we quickly donned waders and tackled up. I gave John a typical North Country wet fly fisher's cast of Snipe and Purple, gold-ribbed Partridge and Orange and Waterhen Bloa. For Jack I tied on a weighted rough olive nymph and on the dropper a rather larger than life March Brown. Jack was to fish the rough broken water at the head of the run, while Jim was to fish the gentler flowing lower half of the first pool. For both, this was a new and exciting experience. On my own cast, I had tied a dry Treacle Parkin, a real favourite of mine. I did not fish immediately, however, as I wanted to ensure that my two friends had first coverage and taste of the water.

I accompanied Jack up to the rough water and watched as he began to fish. We had not long to wait before his rod was arched into the first of his day's sport. Within seconds of this capture, a shout from Jim hailed his first Ure trout. Two fish within the first ten minutes of what was to be the day of days for my Lincolnshire friends. For the next two hours, I was kept busy going from one to the other, as fish after fish was hooked and landed, to the obvious enjoyment of my companions. Though I had not yet made a cast, I must admit I was overjoyed at their success. My first choice of pool had done them proud, with all their captures safely returned to live and fight another day. I had great difficulty getting my guests back to the car for a late lunch.

After a hastily eaten sandwich and a drink, the Lincolnshire enthusiasts were raring to get back to the river. This time, we headed upstream for a good mile and a half to another pool of steady streamy water, with a line of alders shading the deeper farther bank. I knew a good head of lusty trout and, on occasion, a few fine grayling lurked beneath their branches. Jim and Jack then insisted that I show them how I tackled this water with the dry fly, as they had little experience of fishing upstream in fastish water.

Greasing my Treacle Parkin, I waded in and commenced to fish, up-over casting into and beyond the main stream of water, which ran deep and close to the far tree-fringed bank. Here and there, I could see soft dimples of feeding fish. Within minutes, I had my first fish of the day, a nice plump pounder in all its summer glory.

Drying my fly, I covered the next rise and again my Ritz Fario Club rod did its stuff and the hook went home. That afternoon we decided to keep a brace each, even though the limit for this privileged water was ten fish. I could see that the lads were keen to have a go with a dry fly, so I changed their wet casts for a single dry one. I gave Jack a good local dry fly, a Sturdy's Fancy, excellent for both trout and grayling and easily seen, even in fast broken water. Jim was given a dry Olive and he commenced to fish.

I took Jack up to the very top of the beat, where the river narrowed into a steady deepish run, from which I had had many a grand fish in the past. This stretch was only lightly fished, as it was quite remote. Despite the fast current and at times difficulty in seeing his fly, within minutes Jack was into a strong fish. A silver swirl, a flick of the wrist and the reel was singing. A surge upstream, then a dash down river and our best fish of the day leapt into the air, a good two pounder to be sure. So it proved to be, when I eventually slipped the net under its golden flanks. Jack was overjoyed at his first success with a dry fly.

Leaving him to savour the moment, I returned down river to Jim. The smile on his face told me all. He too had relished the joys of capturing a trout on the dry fly. Indeed, he had already put two fish back before my arrival and had lost another two.

It was now late afternoon and, with the shadows lengthening, we took off the dry flies. For our downstream journey back to the car, we fished turn and turn about with weighted nymphs. A dozen or more fish came to the net, before we bade farewell to the river that had given all three of us a most memorable day's sport. It had been perfect in every way and I could not have orchestrated the events any better, no matter how.

My two friends had never experienced such a day in all their fishing lives and were ecstatic. I too was a happy man at their success. I realized how fortunate I was at being able to fish such a wonderful stretch of river. All three of us had memories that would live forever. As we drove home, I am sure my two Lincolnshire friends were savouring their day and looking forward to the morrow, when we planned to return to the Ure, appreciate its beauty and pit our wits against trout and grayling.

After a splendid evening meal, relaxing drinks and pleasant conversation, sleep beckoned. The house was soon silent.

On the Sabbath, we made a slightly later start. Again, the day was fine and prospects for more sport appeared perfect. The stretch of the Ure I had chosen for us to fish was of a more turbulent nature than that of the previous day. It had fast, rocky strewn streams with deep guts and crevices and banks heavily wooded. Wading for the fly fisher would be precarious at times, but there was the promise of an abundance of fish and sport aplenty for the active and brave. This length of water was seldom fished because of its ruggedness. However, though physically demanding, I felt my special guests would relish the challenge.

Commencing at the top of the water, we fished downstream with weighted nymphs on a single leader. Pool after pool was searched by the three of us and the trout readily responded to our offerings. This time we had taken our flasks and lunch in our fishing bags and by mid-day we had reached the bottom boundary of our fishing. We were more than ready for a rest. Jim had done extremely well with eight trout and three grayling. Jack had six trout, one a real beauty, which would tip the scales at two pounds. In between acting as ghillie, I had managed five trout, all around the pound mark.

After a hasty lunch break, we were now faced with fishing back up the water to the top boundary. This was a much harder task, considering the rugged terrain in many parts of our return journey. Jim and Jack persevered with the nymph, whilst I put on a largish Wickham's Fancy, a good floater in fast water. Both my guests caught fish at regular intervals, missing many more, but thoroughly enjoying every moment of this new experience.

We again limited ourselves to one brace each, returning all others, including three large grayling, one of which was a first for Jack. This had been another marvellous, memorable day for my Lincolnshire friends.

On reaching home later that same Sunday evening, both phoned to thank my wife and I for the hospitality they had received and wonderful sport they had enjoyed with the trout and grayling of the River Ure.

In telling this tale of sporting success, I am deeply saddened to relate that within two years of this happy weekend together, Jack died, followed only a year later by Jim. Ten years on, I still miss their smiling faces and good fellowship. Yes, fishing friends are, indeed, very special and my memories of Jack and Jim, two grand Lincolnshire lads, will never fade.

Chapter 23
"A SPECIAL DAY ON FOSTON BECK"

Looking back, it seems a very long time since I motored from my home in Northallerton to Foston, a few miles east of Driffield in the Yorkshire Wolds. I would often link up with my good friend, Tommy Hanson, who had travelled from his Keighley home in West Yorkshire. We always met at Wansford, a village adjacent to the Driffield and West Becks, from where it was but a short four miles to the lower end of the Foston Beck water. For both of us, accustomed to the fast, broken, rock-strewn rivers flowing down from the Pennines, the gentle flow of pure chalk-stream water, with its extreme clarity and superb trout, was a challenge we always relished. I can recall one visit in particular.....

.... I had met Tommy as arranged and we travelled the short distance to Foston Beck. Peering upstream from the little brick bridge, I could already see the soft dimples of feeding trout. No sooner had we tackled up, when Mr Dawson, the keeper, arrived on his bicycle to welcome us to the fishing. He informed us that recent sport had been very good and that the trout were taking the fly well.

I had already tied on my favourite dry fly, a pristine Treacle Parkin. On previous visits, I had enjoyed considerable success with this pattern. Tommy, who had far greater experience of the Foston water, was all set to go with his own favourite, a John Storey. This was a capital local fly, designed by a Kirkbymoorside gamekeeper, John Storey, for the several streams in the Vale of Pickering that flow into the River Derwent.

I offered to fish from the right upstream bank, as I was quite happy to cast with my left hand where necessary. Tommy walked half a mile up the left bank before putting fly to water. I planned to cover all the likely streams and glides between the trailing weeds. Later in the season these can be a problem but this early, in mid-May, growth was not yet rampant.

Eight or nine yards upstream, a large dark shape, hugging the right bank, was, at regular intervals, quietly sipping in flies I could not see. Carefully stepping into the water, I measured my first cast of the day directed specifically at this fish. A perfect cast, or so I thought, but the Treacle Parkin, riding high in the water, was totally ignored. Lengthening my line again, I cast once more, this time bringing the fly back a little faster than the stream's current. A good foot past where I thought the fish to be, my fly vanished in a violent swirl! The first fish of my day had been hooked. Dawson was right. The Foston trout were in excellent condition, for it was some time before I could dip my net beneath the fish's golden flanks. I reckoned it was a good pound and a half, perhaps a shade more, as at close quarters I noted its broad back.

Drying and re-greasing my Treacle Parkin, I continued to enjoy every moment on that lovely babbling stream. The fishing was done at a leisurely pace, but my fly was doing its stuff, fish after fish being deceived by it. Lunchtime came all too quickly and I was loath to leave such perfect fly water. I had two superb trout in the bag and had released more than half a dozen specimens of similar size.

Tommy too had enjoyed an exciting and successful morning's sport, retaining three, the best a real beauty of well over two pounds. Like me, he had had no reason to change his successful fly. From past experience, he knew that the John Storey was good medicine for the fish of Foston.

Dawson had promised his good wife that we would not be late for our lunch. As we had left our homes very early that morning, we hastened to their cottage with sharp appetites. Mrs Dawson was an excellent cook and her culinary delights could not be bettered, even in the finest of hotels. In that little spotless cottage we dined well, listening to her husband relate tales of Foston fish from bygone days and the characters who fished for them. Soon we were replete. After ensuring that our hostess was amply rewarded, accompanied by Dawson, we drove to the upper stretch of the chalk-stream at Lowthorpe, some two miles away, parking near a small wooden bridge.

Here the beck was much narrower, apart from a stretch of some two hundred yards above the mill dam. This length was the home of some really big fish. Dawson, our ghillie, warned us that these large fellows were experienced and wary customers. Casting with the greatest of care was essential for any success. Our chances improved, when in mid-afternoon, fortune smiled upon us and a breeze sprang up, ruffling the water's surface. No longer were we casting to fish we could see, knowing that in the gin-clear water these fish had probably already seen us. With a broken surface, we felt that we had a slight advantage.

It was time to change tactics. Off came the dry flies, which had proved so successful so far, to be replaced with lightly weighted pheasant-tail nymphs, with which on previous occasions I had enjoyed capital sport. Fishing across and down, six splendid fish came my way. The moment I felt the slightest pause or pluck, I tightened. That afternoon's sport was superb. Trout after trout took my nymph. Several fish were lost, including one majestic trout that I estimated to be well over four pounds.

Tommy also continued to bring fish to the net, capturing five more grand trout. His biggest tipped the scales at three and a half pounds ..... a beautifully shaped fish worthy of a glass case.

Time passes all too quickly when one is completely absorbed. When the time came to cross the little wooden bridge back to our cars, we were reluctant to turn our backs on the beck that had given us such superb sport. Foston Beck had certainly lived up to its very high reputation.

Dropping our friendly keeper off at his cottage in Foston, we bid him farewell, pressing that important little appreciation into his weathered work-worn palm before we headed homewards.

Foston Beck will always be high on my list of perfect trout waters, which, over a long lifetime, I have had the pleasure of fishing. Thinking of Foston brings back images of that clear chalk-stream, memories of trout caught and lost and, in particular, the treasured company of Tom, a real sportsman.

Chapter 24
"AN EVENING ON THE AIRE"

As my car sped westwards towards the backbone of England, thoughts of school, school reports and pupils, so uppermost in my mind during the last few hectic days of term, quickly vanished and I began to look forward to running water and leaping trout. I was on my way to spend a fishing weekend with my good friend, Tim Wilson. All was set fair for a "right good do". My tackle, including a portable fly-tying outfit, was safe in the car boot and had been most carefully checked down to the last detail.

On arrival at Tim's house, our conversation, as always. centred round the only topic important to us for the next few hours, namely fly fishing. Inevitably, my hands were soon busy at work, creating a new nymph of my own design, which Tim thought ideal for the low, clear water conditions to be faced that evening on the River Aire.

After an excellent meal, we set off for the river. I had never fished the River Aire and was really looking forward to my first glimpse of the water. Tim intended that we fish into the dusk and beyond into the first hour or two of summer's darkness.

It was nearly seven thirty, when, at last, I waded into the water at the tail of a fast flowing glide, at the bottom of the stretch we were to fish. I was about to make my very first cast to an Aire trout. A good fish was dimpling some ten yards upstream. The Aire at this point is not a wide river and consequently I had to ensure that the fish did not see me. With great care, I measured my cast and the tiny nymph fell perfectly. A split second later, I was into my first fish of the evening ..... a deep thick trout in prime condition! This was a good omen for the evening's sport.

Now, it was Tim's turn, with a fish rising consistently about fifteen yards upstream. Only a long and perfectly placed cast would tempt this fish, lying as it was within inches of the far bank. Tim, an expert caster, took his time to get set and, though his greased nymph fell a few inches short, that fish was round in a flash to take the fly without hesitation. A desperate run downstream, followed by two leaps clear of the water, tired the trout and it was not long before it was safely in the net.

So far, so good. The nymph was proving its worth. We fished carefully through each pool on our journey upstream. In fast broken water, fish took with a bang. On smooth clear glides, the merest check or slight movement of the cast was the signal to tighten. Fish after fish succumbed to our, by now, bedraggled nymphs.

Dusk was fast approaching as we reached the bridge pool. Here we sat on the bankside and had a smoke, Tim a cigarette, me with my pipe. Above us, over the old stone bridge, cars roared past, taking families on holiday to far-off places. This noisy scene was far removed from the peace and tranquility we were enjoying on the bank below.

The nymphs, created only a few hours before, had done their work admirably and surely now deserved a rest. Having planned to fish into the night, off they came, to be replaced by a stouter cast, comprising of a point fly and a dropper. Tim selected a large Brown Owl and a Sedge for this final phase. My choice was a dry Wickham's Fancy on the dropper and a large Butcher on the point.

It was now quite dark, yet our eyes were growing accustomed to the deeper shades of night. Walking up river to the top water about half a mile away, we turned to fish our way back to the bridge. Fishing across and downstream, we hoped to make contact with the big fellows that would, only now, be coming out of their daytime retreats. Tim, a real authority on this type of fishing, was soon into a good fish. This was quickly followed by another, which later proved to be the best of the evening, weighing one pound ten ounces.

In all this excitement, I had the misfortune to snag on a barbed wire fence with my backcast, resulting in loss of my Butcher. The difficulty of tying on a replacement, even with the aid of the now-rising moon, made me realize that my preparations at home had not been fully complete, as the inclusion of a torch would have made the task easier.

Into action again, I heard the heavy plop of a feeding fish half way down a deep smooth glide. Instinctively, I cast in its direction. A second later, I felt a savage pull. If ever a fish hooked itself, this one certainly did and it immediately proceeded to make my reel sing. "A good fish to be sure," I thought, as I gently recovered line. Within moments, a plump pounder was in my net. As I was removing the trout to extract the hook, the fish gave a last vigorous wriggle. Out of my slippery hand it went and back into the water it plunged. Perhaps on another day, such laziness on my part would have made me kick myself. However, on this glorious evening, I had had my full share of wonderful sport and good fortune. Indeed, that lively trout's fight had contributed to my evening's pleasure. Good luck to a worthy opponent!

The weight of my ladened creel told me I should reel in and walk down river, where I found Tim still casting. I think that he too had had a splendid evening and was more than ready to head back to the car. On the way across the dew-soaked meadow and by the light of the moon, we gathered, in our fishing hats, some wild mushrooms. What better ending could there be to a memorable first visit to the River Aire?

We both slept well that night!

Chapter 25
"TWO SEA TROUT UP A TREE"

It was autumn once again and I was going fishing on my three quarter of a mile stretch of the River Wear above Wolsingham. On this particular day, I had invited my dear friend, John Blenkinsop, for him to get to know the likely lies on my water and, hopefully, connect with a fish.

The river was in fine condition, with a good foot of extra water, clearing after recent rains. On the way up to the top of my beat, we came to a large willow, whose branches stretched far out into the middle of a deep lie. In past seasons, I had been successful in taking both salmon and sea trout from here. Landing these fish had always been difficult, as the water was much too deep to wade. Thus, following a hooked fish downstream past the tree was nigh impossible. From my side of the river, I could only step into the water with great care and, hugging the steep bankside, make a very low cast under and across the low branches. If I hooked a fish, I would have to hope for good fortune to help me land it.

Most of my previous captures I had had to tire out below me and then, with the utmost care, draw them upstream and hopefully into the net. Certainly, when the water was at its most productive height, the fish had an advantage and not all I hooked were successfully grassed. Having pointed out all the difficulties to John, he suggested that I give it "a go", before we continued on to the upper reaches. Cautiously, I lowered myself down the steep bankside near the bowl of the willow and into the river. With care, I made a gentle cast across the current and beyond the low branches.

No sooner had my little silver spoon hit the water, than it was savagely snatched by a lively sea trout, which leapt high in the air, hooking itself in the process. It then dashed downstream. I could only keep a taut line and, as my vision was impaired by the willow branches, I had to rely on feel rather than sight. I applied side strain, hoping the fish would swim upstream and beyond the willow's lower branches. Like most of my previous captures, this fish hugged the deep water on my side of the river. Fearing that it would get caught up in the accumulation of brash and tangled roots downstream, I decided that the only way round the problem was to climb out of the deep water, and attempt to scale the tree, transferring my rod through the mass of branches. This proved to be much more difficult than I at first anticipated. As a last resort, I was forced to climb higher into the willow and play the fish from there.

On the bank, John was helpless to give me any assistance. I was now precariously balanced in the fork of a large bough, six feet above the dark, turbulent water. Rather nervously, I began to play the now tiring sea trout, draw it towards me and lift it through a gap in the branches! With great difficulty, I grasped the fish, unhooked it and threw it behind me for John to grab.

Despite my precarious position up the tree, I decided to make another cast over the water beyond me. At my second attempt, I was amazed and thrilled to feel the solid take of another fish. Like its predecessor, this fish hurled itself downstream, but thankfully stayed in the open deep water clear of any danger from bankside debris. It was another sea trout slightly smaller than my first. The fish fought well, but eventually, I gained the upper hand and was able to swing the fish onto the bank. John grabbed it and applied the priest. I had the delicate task of climbing down from the tree, knowing that the slightest slip would spell disaster.

On reaching dry land, we burst out laughing. However, it struck me, that through my excitement and over-eagerness, I had put myself in a ridiculous and potentially dangerous situation. On reflection, our laughter was a sign of relief, for had I slipped, I dread to think what might have happened.

Many times since then, John and I have relived those moments when this ardent fisher landed two sea trout from up a willow tree on the River Wear. What things zealous fishers will do, when they are young, to catch fish!

Chapter 26
"A RED-LETTER DAY WITH MAC"

It was mid-October, early, and I was on my way to pick up my good fishing friend, Mac Kirk, of Harlsey Castle. We were to fish my stretch of the River Wear, above Wolsingham in County Durham. I had already phoned the water meter gauge at Stanhope, which indicated a rise of some eighteen inches above summer level and steady. "Couldn't be better," I thought, as I drove into Mac's farmyard dead on nine o'clock, as promised, to be welcomed by several black Labradors. Mac's two sons, Brian and Graham, were busily attending to the stock. They too were planning to follow us up to the Wear, there to fish a fine stretch of the river about five or six miles downstream of our destination.

Within minutes, we were on our way, having wished the lads good sport. "See you tonight!" we shouted, as we set off northwards on our one-hour journey up to the Wear valley. Crossing the Wear at Witton Bridge, we could see that the river was in fine trim. A lovely whisky tinge to the water augured well for the day ahead.

From the main road, we drove down the grass track to the riverside and the bottom pool, Mac's favourite. I helped him tackle up and wished him well, as he made his first cast. No sooner had I donned my waders, than I heard Mac shout, "Fish!" Hastily, I got the landing net fixed up and sped down to the river.

Mac's rod was arched firmly into a strong fish. Wading in slightly below him, I was poised ready with the net. Three times that salmon was drawn to our side of the fast flowing water, but not quite near enough for me to dip the net with confidence. Mac, an expert, with a long history of salmon behind him, was patient, perhaps much more than I might have been. In due course, his patience was rewarded, as after two more dashes for freedom, I netted the salmon and clambered up the bank with our first fish of the day. Mac's silver Toby spoon was deeply embedded in the fish's scissors. A nice cock fish weighing eight pounds was a perfect start to our day.

With the fish safely unhooked and dispatched, Mac returned to cover the remainder of the bottom pool. I tackled up both my spinning and fly rods, before walking upstream to the middle pool, where two seasons ago I had erected a small wooden seat for the benefit of my elderly guests. This middle pool is one of my favourites. Over the years, it has provided me with many a grand fish and memories of battles both won and lost.

For all the time I have known it, this pool has changed very little, despite the ravages of annual floods. As a result, I know all its likely lies and taking

A fine brace for Mac

spots. Even the elderly sycamores on the opposite bank never seem to alter over the years. They provide shade for the residents of the deep lie on the far side of the main stream. The water looked perfect, as I made my first cast with my favourite gold and silver spoon.

Carefully covering the water step by step, I was nearly through the best of the pool, when the line tightened. My first fish of the day was on. It was no good calling for Mac, as the noise of the rushing water would drown my call for aid. With no obvious snags or dangers, I was able to coax the fish, as yet unseen, upstream towards the head of the pool. Here it would have to work much harder to maintain station and therefore tire more quickly. The fish made several powerful short dashes into the faster deeper water, but at last, I was able to gain mastery and work him towards me. I was now able to get a good sighting of my quarry. "Another cock salmon," I thought. After unshipping my Gye landing net, I applied a steady side strain and drew the salmon over my outstretched net. He was mine!

Looking at my watch, as I always do after landing a salmon, the pointers were on half past eleven exactly. Considering it was late in the season, my capture was in excellent condition, not long out of the sea. In the short time he had been in fresh water, he had travelled far. He tipped my scales at ten pounds.

Returning to the car with my catch, I was delighted to see Mac, coming up river with another fish swinging at his side. This capture turned out to be a fine, freshly run sea trout of five pounds. This lovely fish was a magnificent example of a Wear sea trout.

Mac gladly accepted the offer of a celebratory nip of brandy, before we tackled the next stretch of water. I left Mac to fish the lower deep and excellent holding pool and walked upstream. With my fly rod, I began to fish back down a series of guts and stickles, any one of which could hold a possible taker in this height of water. In addition, I could keep an eye on Mac should he require a helpful netsman.

My Ally's Shrimp was fishing superbly in the peat-tinged water, now flecked with the fitful rays of the pale autumn sun. I was happy with a fly rod in my hand. All was perfect. Half way down the stretch, my line went taut and I tightened into my second fish of the morning. Control of this strong fish would be no easy matter, as many of the deep guts, where resting fish would lie on their journey upstream, had large jagged rocks. By the feel of it, this fish was certainly a salmon and it hugged the deeper water on the far side of the powerful stream. It took some ten minutes of steady pressure to make it move and, when it did, it suddenly leapt high into the air. The Ally's Shrimp was torn out of its hold and the fish was gone! Oddly enough, I did not feel too disheartened and wished my lost fish well on its journey back to its place of birth.

Reeling in, I checked my fly. There was no apparent damage to the jungle-cock cheeks, which I like in this capital fly. Back I went and commenced to cover the water once again, casting rhythmically. Ten minutes later and some thirty yards lower down stream, I had a savage take and my rod bent from the strain of a good fish. It thrashed the surface of the water, as I gathered in my spare line. I set myself in a position from where I thought I could fight the fish and eventually land it. Here the strong currents were to my advantage and soon I was able to slip the net under the belly of another sturdy cock fish, weighing, I estimated, eight or nine pounds.

Mac gave me a congratulatory wave. Placing the fish on the grassy bankside, I put the fly rod to work again. No sooner had I done so, than I noticed that Mac, a hundred yards downstream, was into battle again. Reeling in my fly, I hastened down to do the necessary with the net. This was achieved, but not before many anxious moments when the fish had threatened to go downstream into a maelstrom of white water. This would have spelt disaster. Taking the fish up onto dry land and laying it out on the grass, we looked down on a cock salmon of approximately ten pounds. It was in prime condition.

After this exhilarating fight, Mac was more than ready for a well-earned lunch and rewarding drink. We had truly enjoyed our morning's sport. Six fish on and five safely netted .... not a bad morning's work!

With the inner man refreshed, we returned to the river where we enjoyed further sport in the pleasant afternoon sunshine. I grassed another seven pounder to the fly and lost another in the fast broken water - a fish of some fifteen pounds or more, which I lost at the net. In the late afternoon, a mutual fishing friend, Jonathan Appleby, came down to see how we were doing. He was amazed when we lifted up the car boot lid and he saw the results of our efforts.

Jonathan eagerly accepted my offer for him to take the fly rod and give the stickles a last shot, before we called it a day. The light was now beginning to fade, a time when salmon quite often come on the take. Halfway down the pool, he hooked a fish. Yet again, when it was safely in the net, we saw that we had another six pound cock fish in nice clean condition. Jonathan happily placed this final fish in his car boot.

Darkness quickly descended once the pale October sun had vanished behind the western hills. Our wonderful day was at an end. Bidding Jonathan farewell at the roadside gate, Mac and I headed homewards. When we drove through Wolsingham, lights twinkled from windows. We were wondering what sport Brian and Graham had enjoyed lower down the river. Pulling into the farmyard, we could see that they were back home. This was surprising, as they are usually the very last to leave the water.

Dogs and two young men dashed out to welcome us home and to see how we had fared. Opening the car boot, they were amazed at our catch of six fish. We could not believe their tale of woe, for they had neither seen nor touched a fish all day. Knowing the quality of the water they had fished, we were at a loss to give a satisfactory explanation for their lack of sport, as both of them were excellent fishers.

Though conditions were alike on both waters, we two were the lucky ones Dame Fortune had favoured with fish in a taking mood. Could it be that their water had a batch of running fish much more intent on reaching their spawning grounds whilst the good water lasted? Or was it simply that no fish were there for them to catch? The fact that throughout the day neither they nor we saw fish showing, only deepened the mystery. As Izaak Walton wrote in "The Compleat Angler":

"Angling may be said to be like the mathematics that it can never be fully learnt."

The only thing all four of us were agreed upon was that only the River Wear's salmon and sea trout could give us the answers. However, if by some magic, these magnificent fish did divulge their secrets, then fishing for them would lose its appeal forever.

Chapter 27
"ONCE IN A FISHER'S LIFETIME"

It was a chilly windy day in the November of the very last season of the millennium. I and four companions had arranged to meet and fish for rainbow trout on our favourite trout lake. We were to experience a most exciting and unusual day's sport, which those of us present will never forget. The riparian owner of the lake had granted a two-month extension to the normal trout season. This was a real bonus and was much appreciated by the five of us.

The occasional rainbow, weighing around the pound and a half mark, had already been captured and safely returned to the lake, before Jonathan Bell, the last of our party, as usual, arrived. His late arrival was the subject of much banter. Unperturbed, he tackled up with one of his own special Viva patterns. Approaching the lakeside, he made his first cast of the day.

Amazingly, on his second cast, there was a huge swirl and boil on the surface and his rod was bent double. He was into a good fish to be sure. Reeling in my own line, I unshipped my landing net and went over to do the honours. Our three other companions, John Pateman and Brian and Graham Kirk, also hastened along the bank to add their well-meaning advice to an already red-faced Jonathan. His concern was understandable, because his fly line plus some thirty yards of backing was disappearing into the distant centre of the lake. His nervous tension was probably not eased by the many gibes he had to endure from his watching companions. Retrieving his backing line, only to lose it again, the battle continued for a considerable time, before Jonathan was able to gain some degree of control. At last, we all had a glimpse of the giant fish and inevitably, the conversation turned to the possible weight of the monster. Eight, nine, ten, eleven and even twelve pounds were suggested, along with other comments such as, "Walk back," "Shorten your line," "Keep your rod up," and, "Give it some stick." "Cut his line," was even postulated in the mad excitement of the moment.

After what seemed an age, the giant rainbow was visibly tiring and Jonathan was able to draw it towards me. Using both hands, I was able to dip the net underneath its massive body and, with assistance from John, the huge fish was carried onto the bankside. It was a perfect picture of a pristine rainbow in the very prime of condition. Our congratulations rang in Jonathan's ears. Brian produced his spring balance to give the final and definitive weight - a ten pounder!

After all this excitement, we decided to adjourn for lunch in John's exclusive Land Rover. There we celebrated with a richly earned nip of special Harlsey Castle sloe gin, followed by a fine claret, to accompany our food.

Lunch over, we were all eager to return to the water. Jonathan hastened back to the very place of his earlier triumph. He made his first cast of the afternoon, still using the same successful fly. He was amazed to see it immediately taken by, believe it or not, another giant. His reel screamed and line and backing were once again torn off at great speed.

"You lucky Devil!" John yelled.

"It must be the sloe gin!" I quipped. Three times this gallant fish made strong powerful runs towards the centre of the lake, but all to no avail. Jonathan's tackle held firm. Three times he worked the fish back towards him and, on the last occasion, I was able to dip the net underneath this magnificent rainbow. Victory was Jonathan's!

The fish, a beautiful specimen, looked an identical fish to his first in both looks and condition, and, amazingly, turned out to also weigh ... ten pounds! Two ten pounders within three casts! What a feat - and one unlikely ever to be repeated by Jonathan, or indeed any of us.

But this was not to be the end of the story. Later in the afternoon, this wonderful lake gave up an even bigger specimen. It fell to the rod of Graham Kirk and weighed eleven pounds. It was certainly his largest trout caught on a fly. Like Jonathan, he too will never forget his very last fishing trip of the twentieth century.

Such red-letter days are rare and come perhaps only once in a fly fisher's lifetime, but like all optimists, we live in hope.

Chapter 28
"AN INCH OR TWO MAKES ALL THE DIFFERENCE"

My annual three days on the Mertoun water of the Tweed in late August were a final treat of the Scottish salmon scene, before I returned to school for the autumn term. My fishing companion on this particular trip was Jonathan Bell. We crossed the Scottish border at Carter Bar. Our prayers for rain in the past two weeks had not been answered. All the rivers we had crossed on our journey north were running at their summer level, which did not augur well for our fishing. Nevertheless, we were intent on facing up to the challenge and enjoying our time on this delightful stretch of the Tweed.

After a four-hour journey, we were on the banks of the Upper Mertoun beat, shaking hands with our ghillie, John Taylor, whom we have known for many years. It was always a great pleasure to renew our partnership with such a ghillie. John's knowledge of this stretch of the Tweed is unsurpassed and his advice, expressed in a forthright manner, is always sound. His news was not encouraging, as he told us that only two fish had been caught in the last fortnight. The river was running low, with only one good lift of water earlier in the month. The only encouraging news was that light showers were forecast for the Border region that night, though whether these would make any difference to the height of the water was questionable. As an after thought, John did say that even the slightest of lifts in water level just might stimulate a fish to move.

John made us welcome in his riverside cottage. It was warm and comfortable and, after a hearty meal, we sat and talked until well past midnight. When the whisky bottle was finally drained, we crept into our welcoming beds, there to dream of big salmon that hopefully would be ours the next day. The first night in a strange bed for an over-excited angler seldom results in restful slumber. I was no exception. I had heard it raining very early in the morning, but for how long I did not know. When I finally arose, through the rain-flecked window I could see John Taylor already on the bankside, checking the marker gauge. After breakfast, we sallied forth. Sombre clouds to the west over the Moorfoot and Pentland Hills gave the impression that rain was on its way and John informed us that the river had risen three inches over night. The weather forecast was for a dampish morning in the Border regions, with scattered showers and sporadic sunshine in the afternoon. We were encouraged by John's news, which prompted us to get organized and make ready for the day ahead.

Our knowledgeable ghillie suggested that we fish below the road bridge, downstream to the bottom pool, known as The Kipper - a fine holding pool some two hundred and fifty yards in length, at the very end of the beat. His reasoning was that with even a very small rise in the water level, fish, residing in the Tweed's pools below, might well be stimulated to push up river a short distance. Should this happen, The Kipper would be our best bet for a possible taker.

Jonathan was the first to arrive at The Kipper and, having fished it down twice, sat down on the bank to await my arrival from the pool above. On previous visits in past seasons, I had caught a fish or two from this pool, but not so this morning. However, it had been most enjoyable putting my fifteen-foot carbon fly rod through its paces. My special Ally's Shrimp pattern had looked most inviting as I worked it through the fast stickles, but with no sign of a take.

It was nearly noon when I joined Jonathan and surveyed the pool. The Kipper is a very open pool, fast and deep for about a hundred yards. The main current is two thirds of the way across with a shelving gravel bed on my casting side

I waded in at the head of the pool and began to work downstream. Midway down the pool, my line straightened and I was into a fish. It immediately shot off downstream, making the reel chatter. I hastened to reach dry land and follow its mad rush in an attempt to get below it. Just when I thought that I was at last in command of the situation, the line went slack. The fish had gone. I disconsolately wound in my slack line, with that sickening, forlorn feeling that hits every salmon fisher when a fish is lost. I inspected my treble fly, but could find no sign of a broken hook point, which might have accounted for my lost fish.

"There could be another, Stan. Fish down again," Jonathan suggested, trying to console me.

With little confidence, I waded in again at the head of the pool. Ten yards down, and having just mended the line, I was jolted out of my dejection by the most savage of takes. The reel screamed and my heart beat faster. As I hurried backwards out of the water to regain slack line, the fish broke surface in a violent boil of spray twenty yards below me and dangerously close to the heavily bouldered bank opposite. Once on dry land, I was able to exert some control. The fish made several strong lunges, both upstream and down, but I now felt confident to put on the pressure. Walking further back up the gravel and into the field beyond, I eventually drew the fish to the lip of Jonathan's waiting net. A fresh eleven-pound salmon was safely landed. My favourite Ally's Shrimp treble was firmly embedded in the lower jaw, requiring the use of pliers to extract it.

My morning had given me the two extremes of salmon fortune. With a good fish lying in the grass, I was at that moment a really happy man. Sitting on a bankside tussock, I lit my pipe and smoked contentedly, as I watched Jonathan fish down the pool again and again. It was my hope that he too would savour the joys of a taking salmon. Alas, it was not to be and in mid-afternoon we left The Kipper. We made our way upstream to the Mill Pool, which we fished hard from both banks, but without further takes.

John, our ghillie, who had left us earlier in the morning to do duty on the other Mertoun beats, was delighted at our success, when we all met up that evening. John told us that another fish, a ten pounder, had been caught on Lower Mertoun and he had seen a further three fish head and tail in Middle Mertoun in the late afternoon. This gave us heart for the morrow. That evening we celebrated well, reliving the day's encounters and recalling tales of past fish caught and lost, while all the while the nectar flowed.

The fresh air, our exertions and the whisky ensured we slept soundly that night. After an early breakfast, John gave us the good news. The river had risen another two inches through the night. He suggested we again concentrate our efforts on The Kipper first thing and then fish the Mill Pool and upper streams later in the day. Wishing us a good day's sport, he went on his way to attend to other anglers on the estate's lower beats.

This time we walked directly down to The Kipper. At my insistence, Jonathan had first cast on the inviting water. His fly, an Ally's Shrimp, was identical to the one I had been successful with the previous day. He covered all the water and I also took my turn. Twice we both carefully fished the whole length of the pool, with no sign of a take. After a break for a mid-morning flask of coffee, we again gave the pool our whole attention. Jonathan, casting with care and precision, covered all the likely taking areas, but without a sign of any movement.

"I'll give it a last go and, if nothing shows, we'll head upstream," I said, stepping into the water at the head of the pool. I don't know why, but I decided to fish the fly a little faster, by putting a downward mend into the line and drawing the fly a little faster across the main current. Roughly at the point where yesterday's fish took, my line moved away, straightened and the rod bent. My luck was in again and the battle was on. It was some considerable time before we had a good sight of the fish, as it bored deep and kept to the far side of the main stream.

"A good fish," was Jonathan's comment, as he waited with the net at the ready. The fish eventually tired and began to drift downstream towards shallower water and the fast run off into the pool below. Putting on as much pressure as I dared, coupled with side strain, at last I was able to bring the fish into quieter water, where Jonathan was able to net it. A prime nine pounder was ours!

Despite all our efforts during the rest of the day, fishing the renowned Mill Pool and above, right up to the top of the beat, we had to admit defeat. Two tired fishers, having put their one and only salmon of the day safely in the deep freeze, motored up to the Duke of Buccleuch Hotel in St. Boswells for a well-earned dinner and liquid refreshment.

Our third and last day saw the river down by about three inches. The rains to the west had gone and the sun shone brightly. Fishing was pleasant and I did my very best to put Jonathan onto a taking fish, but it was not to be his day. I knew most of the likely taking lies, having fished the water for several years. However, even the combination of my experience and Jonathan's gallant efforts, was not enough and he had to accept defeat, for that year at least. Perhaps on his next visit The Kipper will be kinder and more generous to him.

Looking back over our three days, I am convinced that the rain gods in Upper Tweeddale, giving the river a couple of inches or so of extra water, had much more to do with my small success than any expertise on my part. I shall never know for certain and this is part of the attraction of salmon fishing. This is why we fishers cross the Border, hoping each year to solve a little more of the mystique of Salar, the "King of the River".

On arrival back home, I gave Jonathan first choice of The Kipper's pair, with both of us vowing to return to the Tweed the following year, to renew our contest with its salmon.

Chapter 29
"A SHOOTER'S TROUT"
and
"A FISHER'S DUCK"

Towards the end of the fishing season, in September, sportsmen, who both fish and shoot, face a difficult decision. Do they have a last fling at the trout and grayling or a first shot at the duck? This was the dilemma that faced George Fawcett, John Kellett and I on one particular Saturday afternoon ....

.... George decided that he wished to fish for trout, while John and I opted for the gun. This pleased our two dogs, Pete and Prince. Leaving George fishing Sandybed Stream at the top of the water, John and I wandered leisurely down river, in the hope of getting a shot or two at any mallard feeding in the margins under the autumn-tinted alders that fringed the riverbank.

As we walked towards the boundary of our shoot, where a small tributary entered the main river, John's keen eye spotted a large trout, which shot out of sight into the bankside at our approach. Handing his gun to me, he took off his jacket and rolled up his sleeve. The two dogs were ordered to sit. John set out to prove to me that, at the age of seventy, he had not lost his skill in the art of tickling trout, learned when he was a youth. Lying on the grass, he carefully reached down into the water and probed down under the bank. Suddenly he swept his hand upward, and there, firmly grasped in his fist, was a pound trout. I was staggered!

An hour later, we were stood waiting at the Holly Bush stream, a favourite stand, with clear views both upstream and down. Suddenly, a flight of some dozen duck came up water, flying extremely quickly. Four shots rang out. Three duck in the water. Dogs at once into action. Pete, John's black Labrador, retrieved two and my little springer, Prince, brought a large drake to my feet.

"I'm sure I hit another!" John exclaimed, as we headed back upstream to the Land Rover. George was still fishing in the tail of Sandybed Stream. He had a wry smile on his face as we approached. Knowing him, we instantly knew that there was something afoot.

"I've been fishing and caught this," he boasted, opening up his fishing bag, from which, with a flourish, he produced a mallard drake. "Now, beat that if you can!" he gloated.

John, slowly and deliberately, undid the straps of his shooting bag. "No problem at all, George," he replied, displaying with pride his pound trout.

Poor old George, his face was a picture of disbelief. We all started to laugh. George explained that the mallard had fallen stone dead at his feet and he only had to bend down and pick it up. It was obviously the duck John thought he had hit earlier, half a mile downstream. This led him to suggest that the duck should perhaps be his, as he had shot it, but under no circumstances was George parting with his best catch of the day and back into his fishing bag it went.

Later, in the local hostelry, we toasted these two unusual captures - a shooter's trout and a fisher's duck! Here was another tale to add to our repertoire to be recounted on convivial evenings spent with sporting friends, while the finest Scottish water flowed freely.

Chapter 30
"THE RESTAURANT"

*Gathering at the restaurant – From left to right:
John Pateman, Peter Storey, John Blenkinsop, Ces Jackson*

Over the last few years, I have always looked forward to accompanying my good friend, John Blenkinsop, on our weekly visits to our favourite inland trout fishery, only twenty miles from home. After a short drive, we arrive in the grassy car park, adjacent to the top lake. This is one of three lakes, all of which we have come to love and appreciate for the quality of the fishing. Situated in a peaceful wooded setting, they are generously stocked with a fine head of rainbow trout. The fly fishing rules are strict but fair and members maintain a very high standard of sportsmanship and respect for their fishery. A strong friendly atmosphere pervades.

The stock of rainbow trout ranges in weight from one pound to over ten and are of the best quality, all-powerful fighting fish, sure to test the skills of even

Nora Pateman with her fine Rainbow

the best anglers. At no time are the lakes ever over-fished by the members. Occasionally, John and I have had the pleasure of all three lakes to ourselves, apart from the presence of the secretary of the fishery, John Pateman. Retired from business, he is as fine a man as you could wish to meet. He spends most of his working days at the lakes, which have become an integral part of his sporting life. All members appreciate his tireless efforts to ensure that we all enjoy the best of fishing. Knowing the lakes so well, John's advice is invaluable. Many a newcomer to the lakes, or a novice, has benefited from his help, given so generously and freely. Such fishers have sometimes been known to find a beautiful, fresh rainbow trout, lying on the grass by the side of their car. John's thoughtfulness is further illustrated by him having seats set conveniently around the lakes. These are especially appreciated by the more elderly anglers, enabling them to rest a while or even to cast from the comfort of the seat.

Occasionally, Nora Pateman, John's sister, accompanies her brother to the lakes. Though in her eighties, she is still a member and is keen to match the men when it comes to catching trout. I well recall one occasion when she did just that ..... catching and netting, totally unaided, a fine seven pounder. I was gratified to learn that she had caught it on one of my special patterns, which I had given her that very day.

Lunchtimes by the lakes are very special. The two Johns, Nora, Peter Storey, a fine left-hand caster of the fly, Ces Jackson, a grand chap and ardent fly fisher from the East Riding and myself foregather at The Restaurant .... a battered, rusty old Range Rover, used by John Pateman to patrol his waters on the estate. Its four doors are fully open and its rear door raised to greet us. We all have our reserved seats. Glasses appear, bottles are uncorked and wine is poured. During a hearty meal, jocular banter is exchanged, as we wine and dine in style. Nora, the only lady present, always appears to enjoy the hilarity and joie de vivre.

These convivial lunches in such beautiful tranquil surroundings are an integral part of our day. Fishing is not just about catching fish. It is also about appreciating the countryside and the company and friendship of fellow fishers. Dining in The Restaurant conjours up memories of good fellowship and laughter and of halcyon days by the lakeside. We six fishing friends are extremely privileged to share each other's company in such surroundings.

Chapter 31
"ALL WENT WELL"

It always gives me great pleasure to see the smiling face of a fishing friend, who has just experienced a memorable day's sport. I had been fishing with my good friend, John Blenkinsop, on our favourite trout lake. From the moment John made his first cast of the day, all went well ...

....It was the middle of May, with warm sunshine and soft breezes, making conditions ideal. After tying on a small copper nymph, one of his favourite patterns, John hurried down to the bottom corner of the lake, to one of his favoured spots. With a gentle south-westerly breeze behind him, his rod was quickly put to work.

Moments later, having tackled up and locked the car, I followed in his footsteps, only to see his rod deeply curved by his first fish of the day.

"It took on my second cast!" he shouted, adding, "It's a good one, I think."

With landing net ready, I waited for John to play out the drama, but not before the rainbow had taken his whole fly line down to the backing. Eventually this powerful fish was beaten and I was able to slide the net under its broad body. A majestic fish, of five or six pounds, was carefully unhooked. Receiving a nod from John, I pointed its nose to the middle of the lake. With a swish of its broad tail, it was gone.

"Well done, John," I commended, "that's a good start. Get going again."

I began casting about thirty yards away, but within moments I was interrupted by yet another excited call from John, indicating a second fish on. I could hardly believe it, but it was so. Winding in my line, I again waited with net poised. The fish, a lively two pounder, leapt out twice, giving John some anxiety for a second or two. Gradually, the rod, in his expert hands, won the contest and I netted the fish in due course. Once again, this capture was unhooked and given its freedom. What a grand start to the day!

Fishing an identical fly to John, I felt confident that before long I too would feel that wonderful moment, when you know that a fish has taken your fly. Despite all my guile and knowledge of the lake and its fighting rainbows, John went on to catch three more trout before, at long last, I made contact with my first fish. After several bursts of frantic action, I netted the rainbow and with all speed returned it to its watery abode.

Moving some distance round the eastern side of the lake and covering many likely spots, I could only manage to tempt and hook one more fish. I quickly realized that I was into a really big rainbow. It gave me some great fun, taking out not only all my thirty yards of fly line, but also a considerable length of backing. It made three powerful runs, before I was able to draw it over the net, unhook it and finally give it back its well-earned freedom. My second fish of the day, I estimated, would weigh well over six pounds, a lovely specimen in the very best of condition.

Meanwhile, John had remained where he had first started, going on to catch a brace of three pounders before lunchtime. John was cock-a-hoop. He had hooked and landed seven fish, all of which had been returned. These, intermixed with other takes missed, due no doubt to the excitement of it all, made for a memorable morning's sport.

The arrival of John Pateman, the custodian of this beautiful lake and the man responsible for the fine fish in it, was the signal for lunch, where we heartily celebrated John's successes.

With lunch over, we decided to move round to fish the western bank. Quite often, we have found that the afternoon's fishing does not match up with the morning's, but on this occasion, John's amazing sport was to continue. No matter what fly he put on to his leader, fish were attracted to it. His day's tally was eleven fish brought to the net, and all were safely returned to live and fight another day. Several more had been hooked but lost. All this had given John a day's fishing that he will never forget.

With only four fish to my name, I could not match my friend's performance on what must surely be his day of days. The smile on his face said it all, as we bid the lake farewell.

For our weekly fishing excursions, John travels a round trip of one hundred miles to be part of a group of fly fishers, who enjoy the challenge of man versus fish in the peaceful surroundings of this select fishery. As John knows only too well, though he had had magnificent sport on this occasion, on his next visit, things might be very different, even in similar conditions. This is the intriguing uncertainty of our sport, for no two days are alike. Nevertheless, John will be hoping that before too long, when he challenges the fighting rainbow trout in this most special of lakes, his success will be such that once again he can say, "All went well."

Chapter 32
"HER LADYSHIP"

The author into a nice Ure fish

In the North of England, we can count ourselves fortunate that many of our rivers and streams are well stocked with the iridescent and graceful grayling. In the golden days of autumn, the grayling provide much pleasure and sport to fishers of the fly. When the trout move to their spawning beds, Thymallus takes over the stream. Now in the pink of condition, she is worthy indeed of being called a sporting fish. It is at this most mellow and pleasant time of year that the hunter of "Her Ladyship" puts a dash of colour at the end of his line.

Grayling are brisk feeders at this time of the year and, though not the earliest of risers, once the sun has warmed the water, the soft dimples of their characteristic rise pattern will be observed by mid-morning. With favourable weather stimulating a good hatch of fly, the rise will continue into the hours of the late afternoon. Streamy glides are their favourite haunts and, being gregarious by nature, once a shoal has been located, sport is usually assured and the angler's day is filled with delights equal to any others in the fly-fisher's calendar.

Dry fly is the order of the day. Bright tags of red, yellow, orange and green adorn the choice of fly, for the angler knows all too well that, like most ladies, the grayling loves a splash of colour. Why this should be so is still, thank goodness, beyond the comprehension of most men. There are, however, occasions when the more sober and true to life patterns, like the Dark Olive and Needle Fly will score better. Nevertheless, in all my years I have seldom found Thymallus put off by a touch of colour in the fly. There are so many celebrated grayling patterns it is, perhaps, unwise to offer a selection. If I had to name but four, my choice would be: Treacle Parkin, Rolt's Witch, Sturdy's Fancy and Wikham's Fancy. But then, on reflection, I cannot really leave out Red Tag, Steel Blue, Apple Green, Hare's Ear and Needle Fly, not to mention Bradshaw's Fancy and the John Storey! What I can certainly do, without fear of contradiction, is to vouch for the grayling's willingness to be an enthusiastic and sporting partner. She is the fish that loves to dice with fancy and play her part in the fly fisher's autumn sport.

I can clearly recall one such day. It was before the deadly salmon disease U.D.N. made its appearance in the River Ure, with drastic results for the grayling population. Mild weather, together with morning sunshine, made conditions ideal for the day ahead.

On reaching the riverside, I could detect the soft dimples of feeding grayling in the tail end of Sandybed Stream. It was here, more than a century ago, that the famous Yorkshire fly fisher, Thomas Pritt, author of the classic "The Book of the Grayling", written in the year 1888, caught his finest ever brace of grayling. I would like to think that this marvellous stream has changed very little in all the intervening years, for it is still a most beautiful grayling habitat. Our thanks must, in no small measure, go to the riparian owners of such fine waters, who have maintained their estates and riversides in such excellent order.

Attaching a tiny Treacle Parkin to my three-pound point leader, I began to fish up the pool from its tail. The river was low and the water only faintly tinged by the peat of the Upper Pennines. Within seconds of starting, the first grayling of the day was hooked and landed. Carefully releasing this typical Ure fish, I dried and re-greased my fly. I then proceeded to cover every inch of that grand water for the next hour and a half, catching and releasing a further seven prime fish. A sharp response to the taking of the fly is the secret of successful grayling fishing. By the time I reached the head of the run, I could see that grayling were back in station lower down the pool, sipping in their autumn feed.

After a break for a quick bite of lunch and a cup of coffee, with my pipe fully primed, I returned to the tail of the pool. I changed my now rather battered Treacle Parkin for another of my favourites, a Rolt's Witch, a more colourful fly. Casting ever so carefully and dropping the fly as lightly as possible on the smooth gliding water, I was soon into the first of many fish brought to the net that afternoon.

The remoteness and privacy of this lovely stretch of water enhanced its rugged beauty. There was I, in my element and completely alone, with the ever-willing grayling in a most obliging mood. Sturdy's Fancy, Red Tag, Green Insect and John Storey were all equally attractive to Thymallus. Only when the sun dipped below the hills and darkening shadows cast their lengthening gloom across the water, did the day's rise cease and the grayling were gone.

With a fine brace of grayling in my bag, I bid farewell to this wonderful stretch of water, knowing that I had been privileged to fish in the footsteps of the great man, Thomas Pritt, who well over a century ago had, like me, cast his fly over this water where the grayling reigns.

Every moment had been savoured and every "Lady of the Stream" had been admired and respected by this happy fisher. Long may "Her Ladyship" flourish in Sandybed Stream.

Chapter 33
"A MORNING TO REMEMBER"

Having caught many salmon and sea trout in the course of a lifetime's fishing, I now take great pleasure in inviting my fishing friends for a day's sport on a small but attractive stretch of the River Wear, where I have been a tenant for over twenty years. Like many in the British Isles, my river is a late running one as far as salmon are concerned. Consequently, fishing is normally restricted to a few short weeks in late autumn, but with a chance of sea trout in earlier months should we experience a wet summer.

However, when the autumn rains do come to our Northern Pennines, the fish quickly fill the river, eager to return to their place of birth. The angler has to make the most of these brief moments, when the fish are coming through on their journey upstream. It is then that my fishing friends receive their annual invitations. Gauging when the water is right is always a bit of a gamble and it is impossible to guarantee that a guest will find everything conducive to good sport. Over the years, I have found that no matter how good a salmon fisher the guest is, it is usually the case that his host catches a fish rather than he. On such occasions, I have wished that the salmon or sea trout on my line had instead been hooked by my friend. This would not only have made his day, but I too would be a happier man.

For a long time now, I have realized that nothing is certain when it comes to salmon fishing. Logic seems to fly out of the window when applied to the vagaries, whims and caprice of the wonderful, yet mysterious salmon. May this situation remain so, for this is why men dream and go to great lengths to fulfil those dreams. John Pateman is such a man.

Recently, I invited him to be my guest. I had estimated that the recent rains in the Northern Pennines would be bringing my river into excellent fishing order. With the water some twelve inches above normal summer flow, conditions for the visit should be ideal for fly fishing, especially if the water was also running reasonably clear. What I couldn't have envisaged was that John's day would be so exceptional.

John motored up from his home in York to my house, arriving dead on time. We transferred all his gear into my car and set off northwards. On arrival an hour later, we drove the car right down to the riverside, a real bonus and were delighted to find the water in perfect fishing ply. We quickly donned our fishing attire and put the rods up. I suggested to John that he tie on one of my special Ally's Shrimp flies, which I knew from past experience would be perfect for the whisky-coloured water we were to fish.

Slipping in at the head of one of the very best pools on my beat, John made his first cast of the morning. I watched him for a while, before departing upstream some three hundreds yards or so to the head of a series of rocky riffles. Over the years, I have had many a fine fish from here. I too had put on a small Ally's Shrimp treble, which looked most attractive in the sparkling waters I was to fish through. No sooner had I settled into a pleasant casting rhythm, when, looking downstream, I saw John's rod bent into a fish.

Hastily, I retraced my steps down the rocky uneven shoreline, unshipping my Gye net as I went. It was some minutes before we had our first sight of the salmon, as it had kept its head in the strong water at the far side of the pool.

"It's a cock fish!" I shouted, as I positioned myself, ready to dip the net when the right opportunity came. Gradually, John brought the fish away from the deep mid-current into quieter water. The fish made several, short, energy-sapping efforts to regain station in the faster water, but John was able to coax the now tiring fish into the shallower stream at our feet. A few seconds later, a salmon of seven or eight pounds slid over the rim of my waiting net. He was a sturdy fresh fish, recently up from the sea.

After congratulating John, I returned upstream to my rod and once more concentrated on covering the waters of the deep rocky pools, in any of which a salmon could be resting on its upstream journey. On many occasions, I have been astounded to find that it is from the small areas of quieter water within this turbulent stretch that I have taken fish. These little deep pots, that over the centuries have been ground and shaped out of the rocky bed by this fast flowing river, are no doubt well known to the native fish. Accurate casting is necessary along this boulder-strewn stretch of water, which, here and there, is over-shadowed by the branches of ancient alder and sycamore, affording additional security to the homecoming fish.

Some twenty minutes had elapsed since John's first encounter, when once again his rod was arched into his second fish of the morning. Reeling in my line, I again hurried downstream to an excited John, who was enjoying every moment of the battle. Again, it was some considerable time before we were able to have a clear sight of this fish, which was most reluctant to leave the powerful main stream and was defiantly shaking its head in the bowels of the pool. The steady side strain applied by John began to tell and, at long last, we had a good view of yet another cock salmon. This one appeared to be much larger than the first. Eventually, the salmon's efforts to reach the haven of the fast deep water lessened and, at last, I was able to slip the net under his body. We admired this fine, firm, cock fish of ten or eleven pounds.

Shaking John's hand yet again, I advised him to complete his coverage of the remainder of the pool, as both salmon and sea trout use it to rest awhile from their upstream journey, having just negotiated a steep incline of four hundred yards of really broken, fast, white water. I pointed out to John that fish are prone to take a breather right on the very lip of the tail end of the run and that he should cover this smooth water with care.

This time, I decided to sit on the seat I had recently erected, which gave a grand view of the whole of the pool. John was putting out a good long line across the gliding tail of this fine water. To my astonishment, his fly was taken savagely by yet another fish. His reel chattered, as the fish dashed madly upstream on the far side of the main current.

"Let him go!" I yelled, as the fish leapt clear of the water. With this fish now safely in the middle of the pool, the fear of it dropping back into the maelstrom of white water below receded and John was able to apply and maintain constant pressure. Despite several brief efforts of resistance, a fine cock fish of eight or nine pounds was brought to the ghillie's net. John could not believe his good fortune, especially as he had experienced a very lean time throughout the season on his favourite Scottish river, the South Esk.

Lunch was taken amid much jovial banter and, despite my own lack of sport, I was delighted with my friend's thrilling morning. Three hours of the most exhilarating fly fishing and three fine cock salmon on the bank do not come often to modern salmon fishers, who cast, ever hopefully, for the majestic "King of the River".

I am confident that John, a fine fisher of the fly, will remember with pleasure his visit to my stretch of salmon water and I am sure he will want to return another year. He can be assured that I will do my very best to organize his day, but I must remind him, that I am only a very small part of the salmon's destiny. What happens next year is largely in the salmon's own domain and not in that of we humans.

As for me, I was really overjoyed that one of my valued fishing friends had, for once, enjoyed real sport. His success made my day. The companionship of a real fishing friend, like the presence of the majestic salmon in my stretch of water, is something very special indeed.

Chapter 34
"THE GREAT CHANGE"

Fishing the Codbeck Reservoir

The years after the end of the Second World War saw many important social changes, which altered forever the lives of ordinary working people. In this post-war period, more and more people found the time to pursue leisure activities. Also, as they became more affluent, car ownership increased. Both these events led to a large expansion in the number of anglers, with the result that our rivers and lakes came under increased angling pressure. However, the increased demand for good quality water to satisfy the needs of peacetime England meant that many new reservoirs were built. Progressive Water Authorities, realizing the huge interest in angling, started to open them up for fly fishing. Reservoirs were stocked with our indigenous brown trout and its cousin from North America, the rainbow trout.

For the very first time, such waters were open to the general public. People new to the sport took up fly fishing and coarse anglers in their thousands discarded the float, taking up the challenge of the fly, eager to sample the fruits of this exciting playground. The sport of still water fly fishing was now available for all and no longer was it the prerogative of the privileged few.

The sport flourished, especially as many of these new waters were within easy driving distance and fishing charges were reasonable. This trend has continued up to the present day. It has been accompanied by numerous innovations. The old traditional fly fisher was to see great changes evolve on these new inland waters.

Tackle manufacturers responded to the growth in demand for more and better tackle and a whole new fishing cult was created. Rods were developed from new materials like fibreglass, carbon and graphite. New reels and types of line were also introduced. Scientific developments in the world of plastics revolutionized the fly fishing industry and modern tackle is well nigh perfect. The stillwater fisher's fly box is a maze of colour, presenting a bewildering variety of choice, so very different from the rather limited choice and subdued hues of the flies used in my youth. That flies in their modern garb catch fish is beyond question. They are another cog in the ever-changing wheel of angling evolution, inspired by the opening up of the reservoirs.

I hope, however, that advances in angling science and technology, do not, in the quest for ultimate perfection in manufacture, completely take away from the fly fisher his skills, artistry and know-how. The fly fisher's art has to be honed and perfected over the years. Furthermore, technology must never take away from fishing its wondrous uncertainty and challenge ... for it is this that gives our sport its magical appeal.

Chapter 35
" FOUR SPIRITS RETURN"

The history of fly fishing abounds in anglers who were masters of their art and became legends, not only in their own lifetime, but also to subsequent generations. I often wonder what the spirits of our past masters would think, if they could return for a day and fish in this new age.

Yorkshire's famous four: Francis M. Walbran, Thomas E. Pritt, John Jackson and Michael Theakston fished both the rivers Yore (Ure) and Wharfe about one hundred to one hundred and fifty years ago. In their writings, they left for us their memories and deep knowledge of their beloved sport of fly fishing. Their works contain not only descriptions of their waterside experiences, but also fine illustrations, detailed observations of fish and fly life and simple classification of their fly patterns. They have a charm and directness that is guaranteed to brighten up the gloomiest of days for the reader. For those of us who have had the good fortune and privilege to fish in our heroes' footsteps, along their favourite haunts, their thoughts and reminiscences become all the more apposite.

Walbran thought nothing of walking and fishing up the river for several miles, fishing for both salmon and grayling and then fishing all the way back, carrying the fruits of his day's efforts in his pannier.

Pritt too would fish for grayling, covering mile after mile of riverbank, ending up in his favourite Sandybed Stream in remote Hackfall. This is a most beautiful stretch of water, which I too have had the pleasure of fishing for many years. I like to think that it has not changed its physical splendour and charm since his day.

How Jackson must have loved the sweet music of the Ure, as it slid peacefully over the weir at Tanfield Mill, bringing refreshing life and energy to the rocky runs and silver streams below the mill race, home of lusty trout and sleek grayling. It is here, in these very waters, that my good friend, Dr Charles Rob, enjoyed many a fine day, fishing the tiny dry flies, which Michael Theakston, himself, would have used all those years ago. Charles would have felt a sense of history when he looked into his fly box filled with the flies that our heroes had created and had unfailingly stood the test of time.

Our four spirits would be overjoyed if they could revisit many of their old haunts in the company of Bill Sturdy, who, until his recent retirement, keepered these waters for most of his working life. Bill, the last of a famous line of river keepers, is truly a man of their ilk. They would be amazed to find and recognize pools and streams that had changed little in all the years between. Shouts of pleasure would greet their recognition of Hell Hole, Mowbray Stream, Holly Bush, Mickley Deeps, Lowsides, Rocky Stream, Sow Dub, Sleagyll and Hatchery Flat as each came into view, with Bill guiding them safely along the way. Each pool would conjure up memories from the past.

Sadly, our doyens of yesteryear would observe that Salar was only noticeable by his absence. They would miss the lively smelt, which was legally fished for in their day. They would, however, be delighted with the present day quality of the resident trout and grayling. Our spiritual guests would certainly remark upon the demise of the local railways, which in their time linked the villages and towns along the river valley with the great industrial cities of Yorkshire. They would be amazed at the sight of a large combined harvester at work in a riverside cornfield, with not a horse and cart in sight.

Our blithe spirits would, to use a good old Yorkshire expression, "be reet capped" with the Range Rover that transported them down to the riverside. They would be astonished by our modern glass, carbon and graphite fishing rods, colourful self-floating fly lines and spools of fine nylon, fluorocarbon and other modern fishing paraphernalia. Even the humble plastic bag, into which most of us today pop the odd brace of fish, would intrigue them. All four would not resist making a cast upon the river with one of our modern fly outfits and, I believe, would be delighted with the experience.

Finally, before the inevitable parting, their day and ours would only be complete after we had adjourned to the King's Head in Masham's Old Market Square. In front of the roaring log fire, we would exchange many a fishing tale and heartily drink a special toast to our mutual love of the River Yore and the friendship of fellow fishers, Then, with a last long shake of the hand and a final wave, they would vanish as quickly as they had appeared earlier on this extraordinary day.

Reminders of Yorkshire past masters

Chapter 36
"FINAL THOUGHTS"

In my mind's eye, I can vividly recall the exhilaration of hooking and landing a fresh run salmon, a native brown trout or a beautiful silvered grayling. I will never forget fish like my first sea trout on Benbecula, my first Nith Springer and my first fish on the Tyne. Etched forever on my mind are fish like the brownie from Sunter's Dub and the grayling from Hackfall's gliding waters.

.....But there is more to fishing than catching fish .....

Fishing the fly is an art. There is nothing to match fly fishing for the thrill and sheer vindication of your skill when you induce a fish to take your imitation fly. There is a quiet sense of satisfaction, when you see a rise under overhanging willows and cast your dry fly inch perfect beneath the branches, watch it glide with the flow and disappear with a swirl.

Like all arts, the skills must be honed and developed over years of practice. Watercraft, the detailed knowledge of river bed, water flow and depth, the effects of the vagaries of the weather, fish holding areas and the correct choice of fly is developed only by experience, perseverance and a willingness to learn over a long period. You never stop learning. My intimate knowledge of favourite stretches of water is a source of deep satisfaction.

So too is the art of fly tying. Over the years, I have found real pleasure in tying my own variations of standard patterns, or even creating new flies. Recently, I created a fly that has become a real favourite among my angling friends. It is a wet fly, a copper nymph, which has proved most successful on lakes and reservoirs. There is no better feeling than catching a fish on one of my own flies, or seeing a friend catch with one of my creations.

I have been privileged to fish in some of the most beautiful locations, appreciating to the full the countryside and its flora and fauna. Picture, if you will, a balmy summer's evening, clouded with myriad insects, dancing over the dimpled pool. The sinking sun, filtering through the trees, dapples the water. A silent lone angler, blending so well into this peaceful setting, casts his fly with precision inches upstream of a rise. Rich is he who finds himself in such idyllic surroundings, for he is, in that instant, at one with nature.

A good fisherman is a keen naturalist, appreciating and observing the wildlife of the riverside. The flash of bright blue, as a kingfisher darts downstream, is a joy. A fly fisher must be something of an entomologist.

Fishing the wet fly involves knowledge and understanding of the nymphal stage of the fly's life cycle, before it reaches the surface and metamorphoses into its imago form. What pleasure has the Mayfly given over the years to countless fly tyers, who have striven to create a perfect imitation, aimed at deceiving the ravenously feeding trout, which relish the annual bounteous feast. A dedicated dry fly fisherman will observe the hatch of fly on the water, so that his choice of imitation dry fly matches as closely as possible those that the fish are feeding on. The John Storey is an excellent imitation of the flies that often hatch on Foston Beck, hence its popularity amongst the anglers who fish this delightful stream.

While quietly fishing, I have often observed some amazing sights. Once I watched a hunting mink come face to face with a mallard and her brood of ducklings. The mallard defended her young with bravery, flapping her wings and placing herself between the aggressor and her family. Undeterred, the feral mink attacked and made off with a duckling. I had witnessed the two opposing sides of nature, the bravery of a mother defending her young and the cruelty of a predator. On another occasion, in Ireland, on the banks of the Blackwater, I was able to watch at close quarters a fox kill a rabbit that initially was holed up in a gorse bush. The fox ran round and round the bush and was so engrossed that it did not see me close by. It flushed the rabbit out, snapped it up and made off. Finally, on Benbecula I was once cut off by seals. I was fishing one of the sea lochs from an island that could only be reached at low tide. As the tide came in, the sea trout moved into the loch, but so did some following seals. Several came ashore and were behind me, causing me great concern, as my route back was now blocked. Eventually, they slipped back into the water and headed out to sea, disappearing as quickly as they had come.

My thoughts often turn to the past. I have a sense that, as a life-long fly fisher, I am part of a history and tradition that goes back beyond the seventeenth century. From those beginnings, this tradition has progressed, through the Victorian era, to the present day. My own heroes, Walbran, Pritt, Jackson and Theakston, are all part of that history, men who had a deep love and knowledge of our noble art.

On reflection, my life has been immensely enriched by all the friends and characters, whom I have had the privilege of meeting in my long fishing career. I have forged deep and lasting friendships, many of which endure to the present day. I would like to thank them all, past and present, for their fellowship and kindness.

It is to these good friends that I pay tribute here.

Copyright

All rights reserved, no part of this book may be reproduced in any form or by any means without the prior permission in writing of the Author.

Designed and Printed by Hillsprint Ltd
The Moor Dalton Thirsk YO7 3JE
Tel: 01845 577313 Fax: 01845 577721
Email: hillsprint@webportal.co.uk